PROCLAMA

Aids for Interpreting the Lessons of the Church Year

SERIES B

Charles Rice
and
J. Louis Martyn

FORTRESS PRESS Philadelphia, Pennsylvania

Table of Contents

General Preface	iii
Introduction	v
The Resurrection of Our Lord, Easter Day	1
Easter Evening *or* Easter Monday	8
The Second Sunday of Easter	14
The Third Sunday of Easter	20
The Fourth Sunday of Easter	27
The Fifth Sunday of Easter	34
The Sixth Sunday of Easter	40
The Ascension of Our Lord	47
The Seventh Sunday of Easter	53

Library of Congress Card Number 74-24958

ISBN 0-8006-4075-6
Second Printing 1976

5790C76 Printed in U.S.A. 1-4075

General Preface

Proclamation: Aids for Interpreting the Lessons of the Church Year is a series of twenty-six books designed to help clergymen carry out their preaching ministry. It offers exegetical interpretations of the lessons for each Sunday and many of the festivals of the church year, plus homiletical ideas and insights.

The basic thrust of the series is ecumenical. In recent years the Episcopal church, the Roman Catholic church, the United Church of Christ, the Christian Church (Disciples of Christ), the United Methodist Church, the Lutheran and Presbyterian churches, and also the Consultation on Church Union have adopted lectionaries that are based on a common three-year system of lessons for the Sundays and festivals of the church year. *Proclamation* grows out of this development, and authors have been chosen from all of these traditions. Some of the contributors are parish pastors; others are teachers, both of biblical interpretation and of homiletics. Ecumenical interchange has been encouraged by putting two persons from different traditions to work on a single volume, one with the primary responsibility for exegesis and the other for homiletical interpretation.

Despite the high percentage of agreement between the traditions, both in the festivals that are celebrated and the lessons that are appointed to be read on a given day, there are still areas of divergence. Frequently the authors of individual volumes have tried to take into account the various textual traditions, but in some cases this has proved to be impossible; in such cases we have felt constrained to limit the material to the Lutheran readings.

The preacher who is looking for "canned sermons" in these books will be disappointed. These books are one step removed from the pulpit: they explain what the lessons are saying and suggest ways of relating this biblical message to the contemporary situation. As such they are springboards for creative thought as well as for faithful proclamation of the word.

The authors of this volume of *Proclamation* are Charles Rice and J. Louis Martyn. Charles Rice, the homiletician, is Associate Professor of Homiletics in The Theological School of Drew University. Before assuming his present post in 1970, Dr. Rice taught at Salem College in Winston-Salem, N.C., Adams United College in South Africa, and The Divinity School of Duke University. Dr. Rice is a graduate of Baylor University (B.A.), Southern Baptist Theological Seminary (B.D.), and Union Theological Seminary in New York (S.T.M.) where he studied homiletics with Edmund Steimle. He received the Ph.D. in American Religious studies from Duke University in 1967. A minister of the United Church of Christ, Professor Rice has served as interim pastor of the United Church of Chapel Hill, N.C., and of Pilgrim United Church, Durham, N.C. He is associated with a movement that emphasized contemporary narrative preaching patterned after New Testament storytelling and is the author of *Interpretation and Imagination: The Preacher and Contemporary Literature* (Philadelphia: Fortress Press, 1970). J. Louis Martyn, who has provided the exegesis for this volume, is Edward Robinson Professor of Biblical Theology at Union Theological Seminary in New York and Adjunct Professor of Religion at Columbia University. He has taught at Union since 1959. Dr. Martyn is a graduate of Texas A & M (B.S.), Andover Newton Theological School (B.D.), and Yale University (M.A., Ph.D.). He has also studied in Göttingen, Germany, on a Fulbright Scholarship. In 1963-64 he was awarded a Guggenheim Fellowship and in 1974-75 he was at the Ecumenical Institute for Advanced Theological Studies in Jerusalem. His publications include *Studies in Luke-Acts* (Nashville: Abingdon, 1966), of which he was co-editor, and *History and Theology in the Fourth Gospel* (New York: Harper & Row, 1968).

Introduction

Amos Wilder was among the first to point us toward the story as a natural speech-form for the gospel. The anecdote, the sort of simple story that people everywhere tell, belongs to the earliest speech of the church and is essential to the community's initial and continuing celebration of the Resurrection. Wilder gives us an example of such an anecdote; Jesus' cure of the blind Bartimaeus at the gate of Jericho (Mark 10:46-52):

> What would this story convey as it was told and retold orally well before there were any written gospels? For its meaning we should put it in the context of the post-Resurrection faith. The believers lived in vivid realization of the time of fulfilment. The Old Testament promises were there and then coming to pass. These were the times when, as we read in Isa. 35:5-6:
>
> Then the eyes of the blind shall be opened,
> and the ears of the deaf unstopped:
> then shall the lame man leap like a hart,
> and the tongue of the dumb sing for joy.
>
> But such salvation in the order of physical well-being was only one aspect of the general redemption. The cure of Bartimaeus was then a dramatic sign of what God was bringing to pass. Like other wonders in what we call the natural order and like certain parables of Jesus it conveyed the truth that God had bared his mighty arm and wrought salvation: being thus a small companion piece to the Resurrection-drama itself. This small anecdote was the Gospel in miniature. [1]

". . . a small companion piece to the Resurrection-drama itself." We could hardly do better in trying to say what we hope for in this booklet and in the stories we hope they will evoke from Christian communities and those who preach for them.

Some say that every Sunday is Easter, and there is no good historical or theological reason to disagree so long as the notion does not lead us to live in that flat liturgical landscape where everything is shouted, or reduced to a muffled beige, so that we hear and see less of the drama than we need. But we can agree that not only every Sunday but the other six days as well have to do with Easter, as surely as Bartimaeus' new eyes celebrate the Resurrection. Our weekday, get-up-and-go-to-work and come-home-and-get-ready-to-do-it-again lives are companion pieces to the day of trumpets and hot-house lilies. And it is there, in our story, that *the* Story finds both its hearing and its continuing, earthy celebration. And there, too, lie the affective sources of preaching. Whether we want simply to pull out the stops and shout "He is risen!" or to try to figure out how to live in the world when the shouting is an echo, we hear and tell both stories. Wilder says that even "the road to moral judgement is by way of the imagination." [2]

1. Amos N. Wilder, *Early Christian Rhetoric* (Cambridge, Mass.: Harvard University Press, 1971), p. 62.

2. *op. cit*, p. 60.

We have tried, in this booklet, to hear as clearly as possible the voices of the early church, and we have tried to hear our own communities speaking their "gospels in miniature." We hope that the end of this will, to some degree, realize the artist's aim: "Not so much to speak as to cause to speak."

The exegete expresses appreciation to a number of interpreters among whom four should be mentioned in particular: Raymond E. Brown for *The Gospel According to John (xiii-xxi)* (Garden City, N.Y., Doubleday, 1970); Ernst Haenchen for *The Acts of the Apostles* (Oxford, Blackwell, 1971); Joachim Gnilka for *Der Epheserbrief* (Freiburg, Herder, 1971); and Rudolf Schnackenburg for *Die Johannesbriefe* (Freiburg, Herder, 1970). I wish to thank Ronald Allen, formerly a student of Professor Martyn's, and now a graduate student in homiletics and New Testament studies at Drew University, who read the manuscript with a holy eros.

Charles Rice

The Resurrection of Our Lord
Easter Day

Lutheran	*Roman Catholic*	*Episcopal*	*Pres./UCC/Chr.*	*Methodist/COCU*
Isa. 25:6-9	Acts 10:34a, 37-43	Isa. 25:6-9	Isa. 25:6-9	Isa. 25:6-9
1 Cor. 15:19-28	Col. 3:1-4	Col. 3:1-4	1 Peter 1:3-9	1 Peter 1:3-9
Mark 16:1-8	John 20:1-9	Mark 16:1-8	Mark 16:1-8	Mark 16:1-8

EXEGESIS

First Lesson: Isa. 25:6-9. It is a fact of the faith and history of ancient Israel that, while God was known always to be King, it was nevertheless necessary for the people repeatedly to experience and to celebrate his kingship. The knowledge of yesterday and of today, important as it was, seemed never in itself to suffice for tomorrow. Note 24:23—"The Lord of Hosts *will* reign on Mount Zion and in Jerusalem."

The present, rather apocalyptic text is the heavenly counterpart, so to speak, of the earthly coronation in the temple of Jerusalem of the kings of Israel. As the recognition of Yahweh's coronation, it has several components: (a) The feast of extraordinarily rich food and fine wine is a symbol, of course, of fullness of life which can be had only in God's realm. (b) The universalism is quite unmistakable. All nations are incorporated in the birth of God's kingdom at Zion. (c) As so often in Hebraic thought, the nations are conceived as being under the domination of angelic powers. Hence a presupposition of the universal establishment of God's kingdom is the vanquishing of these patron angels who have previously blinded the nations (24:21).

This last element now receives a remarkable heightening: not only are the misleading angelic powers put down, but also death itself is swallowed up by Yahweh (cf. the role of Mot [death] in the Canaanite Baal myth). Vv. 7-8 form a powerful part of the poem, evidencing Hebrew parallelism in the words "covering" and "veil," both serving here as symbols of death; similarly "tears" and "reproach." The prophet sees that there is no ultimate celebration of Yahweh's coronation banquet until this last enemy—the enemy of *all* nations and of *all* peoples—has been destroyed. V. 9 is the joyous celebration, not of an annual agricultural "miracle," but rather of this victory over death itself by the one who is the cosmic Lord.

Second Lesson: 1 Cor. 15:19-28. The place of chap. 15 in the epistle is quite clear: it is the climax which has been in Paul's mind from the outset. In the period since Paul's departure from Corinth, a weighty part of the Corinthian church has made an astounding "discovery": They have come to see that the Christ event consisted of nothing other than the revelation of the Essential Man who appeared to die, but whose "resurrection" was actually an illumination of his timeless and spiritual immortality, making clear that he passed through death as easily as one passes through a door. They have also come to see that they themselves share his timeless, spiritual essence, and are thus, in their essential selves, already living in glory. There is no historical drama to human life. Everything is already in hand, at least for those who, like themselves, are truly spiritual (4:8).

Paul perceives clearly that these "spiritual" Corinthians have sacrificed the gift of life which comes "from God," and understandably he does not consider their having done so to be a matter of indifference. At point after point he takes issue throughout the first fourteen chapters. Then, in chapter fifteen, he comes to *the* issue: the death and resurrection of Jesus.

From v. 12 it is clear that reports have reached Paul informing him that some of the Corinthians deny "the resurrection of the dead." From this we can rightly conclude that they affirm *Jesus'* resurrection, but only in the sense indicated above: his "death" was a momentary passage, and his "resurrection" was a revelation of his timeless essence. That means, in turn, that the thought of a general and future resurrection has no meaning to them. Hence Paul comes, in vv. 20-28, to the crux of the matter, which he expresses to some considerable degree with the terms "first fruits" (v. 20) and "order" (v. 23). Notice also the studied use of the word "then" (vv. 23-24). The coming of Christ (cf. Gal. 4:4), his death, and his resurrection are not points at which one may get a glimpse of a timeless essence. They are in fact events in God's overarching deed of re-grasping the world under his sovereignty. *And*, the whole of that overarching deed is by no means already accomplished. Christ's resurrection is only the "first fruits," the surety of God's ultimate victory. It is not an isolatable event, which may be studied in and of itself. It is, on the contrary, the beginning and guarantee of "the resurrection of the dead" (v. 21), that is to say, of the general resurrection. As such it involves us all, whether we know it or not. Paul has no doubt that in Christ "*all* shall be made alive" (v. 22).

But, again, he does not speak of the general resurrection as something which has already been accomplished. All *shall be* made alive; each in his own *order* (v. 23). Christians, and, in fact, all of creation (cf. Rom. 8:18 ff.) are not yet at the goal. Hence the temporal use of the word "then." In short, Easter is not the end, but rather the beginning.

The beginning, precisely, of what? The beginning of God's new creation (2 Cor. 5:17), which he is bringing into being by vanquishing all hostile and enslaving powers (v. 24), the last of which is death itself (v. 26). It is sheer folly to deny the existence and potency of these enemies (4:8). Nor are they overcome by one's coming to a knowledge of his own essential self. It is Christ who overcomes them, and he is even now doing that, in order finally to deliver the regrasped world, and even himself, to God. God's new creation is, thus, not a *thing* that is completely given; it is, rather, the unfolding drama of Christ's past in the reality of death, and of Christ's presence as risen Lord, and of Christ's future as the one who continues to bring under his subjection the tyrannous powers in human life; and ultimately it is the drama which is our liberation because it ends in God's being "all in all."

Gospel: Mark 16:1-8. We begin by noting the broader context of this paragraph. To a large degree the Gospel of Mark is stretched out on the background of extraordinary dramatic tension. Already in the first chapter, the reader senses that the coming of the Spirit on Jesus impels him into tense conflict with the evil spirits which imprison human beings. Jesus himself speaks of the necessity first to bind the strong man (Satan) before he can enter his house (the orb of human sin and enslavement) and plunder his goods (free those who are possessed). Nor is the conflict simply an otherworldly one. Just as Jesus embodies the liberating power of God's new age, so many of the religious and political authorities embody the enslaving powers of the old age. Consequently it becomes clear that the struggle will find at least one of its climaxes in the real and painful, yes, horrible death of Jesus (3:6). The authorities of the old age cannot tolerate this man. The preservation of their hegemony necessitates putting him out of their world.

In the passion narrative itself there are weighty symbols pointing to the fact that Jesus' death is not an "unfortunate incident," but is rather *the* point at which the two ages collide. One pair of these symbols is provided in 15:33 and 16:2. In these two verses Mark is not giving his readers the time of day; he is bearing witness to the eschatological conflict. There can be little doubt that for Mark the darkness at the crucifixion stands for the ultimate show of strength on the part of the "powers of darkness," the demonic, religious, and political forces of the old age with whom Jesus has been doing battle through the whole of the gospel story. Similarly the perfectly "natural" dawn of a new day (16:2) is in actuality a sign of the victory of the inbreaking kingdom of God, the new age. Mark's attentive reader already perceives that God does not intend to leave Jesus in the grave. But, what form, precisely, does God's victory take?

One will not want to forget that the victory has already taken proleptic form in the course of Jesus' life: the possessed have been liberated, the sick have been healed, the hungry have been fed, the ignorant have been taught the words of life. These forms of victory remain the good news which Mark calls the good news of Jesus Christ (1:1). The passion narrative shows, however, that the drama is yet larger, the opposition yet fiercer and more desperate, and the dimensions of God's kingdom yet more comprehensive. "The last enemy to be vanquished is death."

Thus our paragraph unfolds. The women come in order tenderly to perform the anointing rite due the dead. But the body is not to be found. Instead they encounter an angel who announces to them that Jesus of Nazareth (the really crucified one) has risen! God's victory takes the form of the vanquishing of death.

But there is more. We are at one of those points at which careful literary criticism and synoptic comparisons bring out weighty dimensions of the text. One notes, first, that Mark 16:7 repeats a promise made by Jesus in 14:28. That fact in itself gives a strong hint that the verse may be Mark's redaction. Second, one notes that 16:8 follows more easily on 16:5-6 than on 16:7. Fear is a standard reaction to an angelophany.

Having seen the angel and having discovered the empty tomb, the women flee in fear.

If Mark provided 16:7, what was his intention? Comparison of Mark 16:7 with Matt. 28:7 will show how Matthew understood the verse. He takes the promise, "there (in Galilee) you will see him," to point forward to the appearance of the risen Lord to his disciples on a mountain in Galilee (Matt. 28:16 ff.). But is this necessarily Mark's intention? Pondering the question will remind us of the remarkable fact that Mark is content to close his Gospel without narrating an appearance of the Risen One. (The question of the genuineness of Mark 16:9 ff. has been recently reopened in an impressive way; yet in what is written here the secondary nature of these verses is assumed.) To what, then, does he intend to point with the promise of 16:7?

There are good grounds for seeing it as a promise of the parousia. Perhaps, however, one should not compel the text to yield a single level of meaning. The promise may refer both to a resurrection appearance and to the parousia. In that case, we see that the form of God's victory encompasses the gospel story, and Jesus' resurrection, and also what has been so suggestively called in our time "the future of Jesus Christ."

HOMILETICAL INTERPRETATION

The momentum of this weekend may leave us speechless. One event converges upon another from Thursday to Sunday, and the pace tries our powers. When were sorrow and joy, alienation and love, death and life so impacted, or when were men and women called on to find words to accompany such events? Do our musical and homiletical extravagances, services and sermons as overdressed as the congregation, betray our feeling of inadequacy?

As a matter of fact, standing speechless before the Easter event may be the best preparation for preaching today. Günther Bornkamm suggests that it may be so:

> The contrast between what men did and do and what God has done and accomplished in and through this Jesus, belongs . . . inalienably to all the New Testament testimony of the resurrection. In this the first Christians do not consider themselves in any way as confederates of God and comrades-in-arms with their Lord, as we might put it. They regard themselves as those who have been conquered, whose former lives and beliefs have come to naught. The men and women who encounter the risen Christ in the Easter stories, have come to an end of their wisdom.[1]

What is the mood of Easter morning? Why bother to get up before dawn if not to keep a vigil and, as befits mortal flesh, to keep silence for a time and to stand in fear and trembling?

That is the mood which John Killinger, too, suggests for moving toward the pulpit today. He warns us away from trying to *prove* something, as if

1. Günther Bornkamm, *Jesus of Nazareth* (New York: Harper & Bros., 1960), p. 184.

we had to roll the stone away. God has done it already, as he has created and continues to create his alleluia-singing people:

> In the church, then, as the community of the Restoration, the preacher is not called on to be an orator or public advocate. He is instead a listener, a mediator, a friend, a fellow, a catalyst. And he is all of these primarily as a man among men who is always seeking more and more wholeness for himself and is never inhibited about saying this to his congregation, that is responsible for the sense of Restoration, and, by that token, for the preaching of the church as well.[2]

When we feel that way about it, that it is God's doing, that the resurrection has made this church in the first place, and that the restoration to new life is a tangible kind of fact that people know today, then we can enter into the joy of this day.

1 Cor. 15:19-28; Isa. 25:6-9. We arrived at the church early, before eight, on that day of high celebration. Someone had been there before us. That is the way it happened on Easter Day, isn't it? Some Easter angel had done it, scooped us and said it all before we had a chance to put on our black gowns and get up in the high pulpit and announce loudly that he was risen and that everything was therefore OK. Speak of non-verbal communication and standing there upstaged in your wordiness! There it was, smack in the middle of the narthex, just sitting there in all its battered rusty brown and sunshine yellow glory, stark and beautiful as fine linen lying on a stone floor. It was a garbage can which had been run over by the truck a dozen times and flung aside empty on a hundred times that many Monday mornings. Now, at the gate of heaven it overflowed with six or seven dozen chrysanthemums. "Christmas anthems" we used to call them. Easter alleluias at least.

Easter is God's day. It is hard to find metaphors as apt as that unlikely bouquet, but that *is* what the day is about. It may be possible on other days and in other circumstances to speak less theologically, but when we come to the crucifixion of Jesus, the dispersion of his followers, and the general gloom of what appeared very likely to be a lost weekend, only to receive from these same defeated people the witness of Jesus' resurrection, like all of the lections for today we can only witness: "It is the Lord's doing, and it is marvelous in our eyes."

Paul could not be clearer: everything depends upon the resurrection of Jesus, and it is God who has raised him. Where we might be inclined to point to the success of the church or even of our own ministry as "proof" of the resurrection, Paul takes just the opposite view. If God has not raised Jesus from death, then he is not at work in him or in us and it is all a washout. Paul, however, does not tarry over such speculations: "But in fact Christ has been raised from the dead . . ."

Paul is pointing to God's adequacy for his people: God has not left his Holy One in death, and he will in the same manner deliver his people from the "last enemy." Paul almost personifies death, and he hangs a great deal

2. John Killinger, *Leave It to the Spirit* (New York: Harper & Row, 1971), p. 162.

on God's overcoming the threat which it poses. We can appreciate the meaning—and the threat of meaninglessness—attached to the death of Jesus. Here is the innocent being put to a criminal's death at the hands of the guilty. The death of Jesus is loaded with our deepest moral questions. But as to death in general, would we wish to put the matter just as Paul states it? Is death for us the last (ultimate?) enemy of mankind? In an overpopulated, underfed world, is the death of a person at home in bed among friends at the end of a long life an "enemy" at all? Where is God winning his victories in our world? Where is Jesus Christ crucified? Where is he vindicated? Where in our day do we see the salvation of the Lord? Is there being realized among us today the hope of Isaiah for plentiful food, good wine, and the Lord's glory which will dispel the cloud that covers the land? For what do we wait, even on this side of Easter?

The earliest church, even while rejoicing in the resurrection, waited for the parousia. We can be sure that Isaiah's cultic feast which celebrates God's kingship is at the same time a feast of waiting for the victory yet to come. Such a feast is always a having and a not having, a foretaste. That is certainly the mood of the central feast of our faith in which we remember, rejoice, give thanks, and yet wait for more to come. Having, yet not having, filled, yet hungry, saved from death, yet dying. Has that way of waiting changed since the first Easter? Do we not wait still for Isaiah's day of peace and plenty and the hope that Jesus' victory will indeed have its final fruition in us and all peoples? To have God's blessing is to wait for more, just as to celebrate God's greatest day, this Easter, is to wait still for the day of the Lord. "Blessed are they that hunger, for they shall be filled."

Mark 16:1-8. What a picture of surrender, of the first dawning of hope, of not daring to believe. It is like a person who has been very ill who takes a tentative walk and feels something in the air and in the forgotten pleasure that he takes in it that he is getting well, and yet he walks carefully.

Mark's story of the women coming with fragrant oils to the garden tomb evokes in us quietness, vulnerability, even passivity. Here are people who have come to the end, who have done all that they can do. Now they come to the tomb with their pitiful offering not even sure that they can get to his body to make this last gesture.

Then, to make us feel even more deeply our helplessness, Mark fixes our attention on the great stone at the entrance of the tomb. The monolith is blunt fact, certain death, the way things have always been and always will be, the undeniable power of the state, our doubts, our not daring to hope. The stone preoccupies the women.

Then the stone is no longer there. How else do you handle a stone as huge as that? It is simply rolled away. The women enter the tomb and the messenger tells them what they can plainly see: "He is not here." The stone is removed, and Jesus is not here. The assurance that he has been raised and that he is going before them into Galilee seems lost on the women, for at the end of Mark's account, they are both silent and afraid.

To what degree do the people to whom we preach today experience the Easter message in this way, or would they do so if we could get past the twittering birds and sentimental optimism of a haberdasher's Easter? Why do we have a story like Mark's at all? Does such a story complement Paul's more straightforward catalogue of witnesses to the resurrection (cf. 1 Cor. 15:3-9)? Mark is not so much interested in proving the truth of Jesus' resurrection as in evoking the sense of awe and mystery surrounding it. We might do well to balance, at least, the more blatant and trumpet-like announcement with this tradition.

In his understatement of the story—Mark does not give us a resurrection *appearance* at all!—the Gospel writer suggests, in his own way, that this is *God's* doing. Who can help but tremble and keep the holy silence? The Russian Orthodox Church, before it displays the full glory of its celebration of the resurrection, keeps the Easter vigil. It is in that mood that Mark brings us to the tomb where we feel in the emptiness of the place our absolute dependence upon God. Perhaps we are never closer to the Easter celebration than in that fearful, hopeful, vulnerable mood in which we wait for God to move the stone which is too big for us.

The major celebration of Easter among the Moravians of Winston-Salem, North Carolina, takes place in the cemetery, or "God's Acre" as they call it. There the saints have been buried for generations under simple white stones which bear testimony by their simplicity to the faith of a plain people and to the "democracy of death." Between the love feasts of Holy Week and Easter morning the people come with brushes and pails to scrub the stones, and on Holy Saturday every stone gets a bouquet of fresh flowers. And then on Easter Day, before dawn, the whole community meets at the church and to the subdued sound of brass bands, they march to the cemetery. Among the orderly rows of marble, in the very teeth of death, they celebrate the resurrection of Jesus Christ from the dead. It is as if that were the only proper place to have such a celebration, out there among the tombs where death is unavoidable, even in the dawning light of an April day among the people's flowers that have not yet begun to wilt. It is the *mood* which strikes a worshiper there. It is not brassy: even the bands sound slightly cold as they play antiphonally from hill to hill. There is hardly a sermon at all, mostly just the familiar words. It is all understated, and there is about it a quiet waiting, for the sun to come up, and for more.

Easter Evening *or* Easter Monday

Lutheran	*Roman Catholic*	*Episcopal*	*Pres./UCC/Chr.*	*Methodist/COCU*
Dan. 12:1c-3	Acts. 2:14, 22-32	Acts 2:14, 22-32		
1 Cor. 5:6-8				
Luke 24:13-49	Matt. 28:8-15	Matt. 28:9-15		

EXEGESIS

First Lesson: Dan. 12:1c-3. Who are "your people"? And why are they in need of deliverance?

The Book of Daniel was written shortly before 164 B.C., in a period when external political and military might (the Seleucid ruler Antiochus Epiphanes) got linked up with the attractiveness of Hellenistic culture to threaten the preservation of the Jewish faith. The author was one of the Chasidim who initially greeted the Maccabean resistance as God-inspired, only to find that it too unfolded unidimensionally on the humanly political and military level. At the time of writing he lives in a group of faithful Jews who refuse to defile themselves "with the King's rich food" (1:18), as they search for the meaning of a brutal history which finds them not infrequently mourning the death of loved ones slain by the Seleucid army.

In order to read the author's book from the "inside," therefore, we need to imagine ourselves hiding from Seleucid soldiers by huddling together in a Judean cave with fellow Chasidim who, in the face of such brutal experiences, have come to believe without a doubt that history is doomed to remain an enigma both to persecuted and to persecutor if their eyes are fixed solely on what they perceive to be events transpiring on an earthly stage (2:10; 2:27; 5:8, etc.), as though there were a human orb from which God were absent. These Chasidim are sure the enigma is interpreted only when God grants stereoptic vision, enabling one to see both the (dependent) earthly stage and the (determinative) heavenly one. Such God-given stereoptic vision, is, in fact, the genius of "apocalyptic," and the seed bed in which the crucial hope for resurrection took root and grew. Antiochus Epiphanes proudly saw only the corpses of the defeated weak ones, and, correspondingly, he saw only his own might and glory. Moreover, he successfully invited seducible Jews to see exactly what he saw. However, to the suffering and martyred Chasidim God granted (and grants) quite a different (angle of) vision, enabling them to see "that the Most High God rules the kingdom of men" (5:21; cf. 11:32b) and that while they themselves may "fall by sword and flame, by captivity and plunder" (11:33), God and his purpose for them are *never* in fact defeated. He sends a hand to write on the wall words which spell the doom of monoptic earthly rulers who preen their own feathers while violating their fellow human beings (chap. 5). And *in his time* he will deliver the

Chasidim who are living, will raise to everlasting life their comrades who have fallen, and will raise to judgment the persecutors and their accomplices. It is, thus, not surprising that Daniel sees a general (or corporate) resurrection, for the hope of resurrection is not at all at home in an individualistic frame of reference. It is, rather, part of God's word to the otherwise hopeless enigma of corporate human destiny in the face of evil.

Second Lesson: 1 Cor. 5:6-8. None of Paul's letters shows more clearly than 1 Corinthians the interpenetration of what we call "ethics" and what we call "theology." In the course of the first four chapters Paul confronts the Corinthian Christians with the essential dimensions of their near apostasy precisely by indicating God's present and powerful activity in areas where they thought they were themselves doing the deciding (recall the monoptic view of Daniel's persecutor, and, more important, note carefully the studied imbalance of 1 Cor. 1:18; the jolting penultimate clause of 3:23; the scorn Paul pours on the Corinthians' discriminatory powers in 4:3). The *Christian* gospel (2:1 ff.) does not describe the movement from a heteronomous to an autonomous conscience, thus enabling human beings to celebrate themselves and their potential with equanimity (4:8). *That* gospel is rather God's powerful action (1:18) in and through the ignominiously crucified Christ, and in and through apparently weak and foolish apostles in whose daily death for others the truly liberating life of Jesus is effectively manifested (15:31; cf. 2 Cor. 4:7 ff.).

Now, in chap. 5, Paul turns to a specific instance of the Corinthian tendency to celebrate naked human vitality: A member of the church has "shacked up" with his stepmother, and a good many of the Corinthians are proudly boasting over his and their liberation. Paul's horror (focused considerably more on the boasting than on the deed) reveals again the relation of *the indicative* of God's powerful invasion to *the imperative* of ethical command: "*Cleanse out* the old leaven . . . just as in fact you *are* unleavened." *The* event has now occurred. At Passover time, the time when Israel's hopes for deliverance were brought to fever pitch, God in fact delivered us from the reign of malice and evil. The community is already unleavened (cleansed) from the power of self-deceit by Christ's paschal death. Paul, therefore, in *exhorting* them to celebrate not themselves, but rather the Paschal Easter Feast of the crucified one who is God's power and God's wisdom (1:24), exhorts them only to be what in fact God has already caused them to be: people who are singularly focused not upon themselves but upon God's truth. Good Friday and Easter form the locus of the transforming miracle which is "in us" only because God has placed us "in it."

Gospel: Luke 24:13-49. No single chapter in Luke's two-volume work is more revealing of his theological commitments than this final one of the Gospel. He carefully structures it from three primary literary units, the story of the empty tomb (23:56b—24:11), the Emmaus story (vv. 13-35), and the story of a Jerusalem appearance (vv. 36-43). In and around these traditional units Luke accents certain points of crucial importance to him. In each he portrays a movement from perplexity and consternation (vv. 4, 21, 37) to the granting of a new hermeneutic (vv. 5b ff., 27, 45) and climactically to the knowledge of Christ's resurrection (vv. 31, 34 f., 46, 52). God's lordship over all of history (recall the First Lesson from Daniel) is now grasped in the new hermeneutic which focuses the message of scripture in three infinitives (vv. 46 f.): The Christ is *to suffer*, and *to rise* from the dead (Luke's volume no. 1); and in his name forgiveness of sins is *to be preached* to all nations (Luke's volume no. 2). The third infinitive is no less a part of God's effecting his lordship over history than are the first two. But where is he to find those who will do the preaching?

This question leads us back to the second of the traditional units, the famous Emmaus story, which may have a new ring when read on the heels of the two lessons. Cleopas and his companion are not strangers to the kind of Chasidic hope which burned in the breast of Daniel. Moreover, for them, this hope has received a powerful impetus in Jesus' preaching and deeds, so that they have begun to suppose that God's deliverance and vindication are to appear momentarily (cf. Luke 19:11). At this point comes the Pasch and the taut eschatological stretching of the nerve of hope. And then what? The bubble bursts, the picture shatters, the hope evaporates in the merciless afternoon sun. God's prophet of imminent deliverance is himself arrested and summarily executed.

At this juncture one supposes that the disciples could have returned to Daniel *et al.* to find comfort in the hope of resurrection. "Together with other fallen martyrs," they could have said to themselves, "Jesus will be raised in the (general) resurrection." But God puts his stamp on this eschatological hope, while also transforming it. He raises Jesus from the dead *now* and sends him to the distraught disciples in order to make them into his witnesses who shall march in the power of the Spirit from Jerusalem to the ends of the earth. "To rise" is the middle of the three programmatic infinitives (vv. 46 f.), binding the other two together. It is the risen Lord and he alone who opens eyes (v. 31) and minds (v. 45), so that persons are transformed from disciples who have imperfectly learned Jesus' teachings into witnesses through whom God in fact effects his lordship over the whole of human history (Acts). The resurrection of Jesus is not an isolatable event, a freak happening which may be investigated in and of itself, or even a *private* warming of the heart to which an individual may return over and over. It is God's re-creative deed by which he inaugurates the communal transformation to life which is his will and intention for all humankind.

HOMILETICAL INTERPRETATION

These days if you had seen what Luke's two travelers had witnessed you could more easily divert yourself. There is always television, which numbs us to human suffering by showing it every day and then helps us forget about it by flip-of-the-switch distraction. How much can be put out of mind, and how much lost, sitting in overstuffed chairs stuffing ourselves with our minds completely engaged by the cool medium? It is hard to imagine anything that could be reported on the Friday evening news that we couldn't live with through a weekend of electronic diversion.

We may, nevertheless, be able to enter into the story of Cleopas and his friend as they leave Jerusalem where hopes have risen so high only to be brought so low. Where do we go when our hopes have been dashed, when a beaten up garbage can expresses us? It is bad enough when your private ship of dreams runs aground, but what do you do when the *world* you have come to believe in falls down around your head and the best people you know suffer? If we stopped to think about it we would probably count ourselves lucky to have one friend to walk along with us and talk it out. Luke offers us more even than that, and the other lections point toward finding our real identity and making sense out of what happens by seeing God at work.

Dan. 12:1c-3. Who could fault a newscaster for signing off every weekday: "And that's the way it is"? What else is a news reporter to say about the sorry scene he must survey day after day? Only occasionally, when some poetic reporter forgets the news and turns the camera on someone who has stopped watching television and lives off by himself or herself someplace close to the earth or animals or God, do we get some slight view past the way it is to the way it really is, or at least might be. And we wish we could go "on the road" more often! But, for the most part, to read the newspapers and watch the evening news is to become what Richard R. Niebuhr calls "radial man," who is constantly hooked up by the media to the sorry show of the way it is.

That is not the way it is with the writer of Daniel. The writer is in a state of mind not unlike that of a black slave singing about freedom to the rhythm of chopping cotton. What this Jew has seen in Jerusalem does not let him rest, and his imagination is stretched to its limits by the disparity between the events of the day and his faith that God is the Lord of history. Vision, more real to the prophet than the events that a newscaster would report, moves him to hope and to chaste living. He speaks of the "book," in which are written the individual names of all those who have kept themselves unsullied. Even those whose bodies have been reduced to dust will awake and will shine as the stars. These are the "wise" who know that the way things appear on the bald face of history is not the way things are in God's economy, and that to do right and to try to turn others to righteousness is not, even in such times as when the high altar is defiled, a waste of time.

Here is John of Patmos, holding out for a new heaven and a new earth on the very island from which the Caesars quarried stone for their eternal city. Here is the dogged hopefulness of Dilsey in Faulkner's *The Sound and the Fury*, as she is able to endure the world because she has seen "the first and the last." Here is the church, as human as underwear and sometimes as quaint as prunes, demonstrating in its life that the kingdom of this world is become the kingdom of our Lord and of his Christ.

1 Cor. 5:6-8. Here again we are pressed by the questions: What *is*? Who are *we*? Paul takes on a case of immorality in the church, and the passage seems a bit foreign to us. When did we last see anyone excommunicated or "churched"? It is not so much the details of the matter (which the makers of the lectionary have conveniently omitted) or Paul's high standard of church discipline which concerns us on this Easter evening as his rationale for purity of life among Christians. Paul says quite simply that our behavior is part and parcel of our celebration of this holy festival.

As a matter of fact, Paul says, you *are* free from sin, "unleavened." That's the way it is! Morris Niedenthal calls it "the grammar of the gospel." You *are* set free in Christ, forgiven and redeemed; now you *can* behave that way! We are prone to reverse that grammar, to make the imperative prior and to turn the indicative toward the conditional. When we do that, "God is good, therefore be good," becomes "Be good, and then God will be good to you." But Paul never falters in this matter. It is what God has done which is decisive. Paul spends the first eleven chapters of Romans showing how God's grace overcomes our sin, abounding all the more where our sin abounds, and it is only in chapter twelve that he moves to "Therefore, I beseech you, brethren, to present your bodies a living sacrifice . . . by the *mercies* of God . . ." As God raised Jesus from the dead, so he acts in unconditional grace toward us, overcoming by his power both sin and death. It is from that knowledge that we act, not in fear but in the confidence of people who celebrate *God's* triumph at Easter. Edmund Steimle has well said: "Behind and beneath the summons, the call to commitment, the charge to act responsibly, must be the word of the gospel addressed to the 'need of man for a basic security from within which he can be free for change.' "[1] Does not the whole ethical imperative of our faith unfold from this day? "And every man that has this hope in him purifies himself, even as he is pure" (1 John 3:3).

Luke 24:13-49. It is a long way from the opening of Luke's closing chapter to its end. The evangelist begins with Mark's story of the fearful women and ends with the disciples embarked on a mission to the world. Three distinct accounts move us along this road: the empty tomb, the travelers to Emmaus, and Jesus showing his feet and hands to his disciples in the upper room. These stories meet us in the various moods in which we come to Easter. But in the whole of the Gospels, does any story help us to celebrate more than Luke's narrative of the two friends who, even as they talk it over, are overtaken, fed, enlightened, and sent running with good news? Don't we still walk along wondering, speaking of snowed-under hopes, trying to make sense of it, at least trying to be with each other?

1. Edmund Steimle (ed.), *Renewal in the Pulpit* (Philadelphia: Fortress Press, 1966), p. xii.

And then he stands beside us, opening the scriptures and breaking the bread and warming up hearts that are cold and giving life to spirits as dry as a navy bean. This story says a lot more to us than some would say if we were in the shoes of those two heads-down travelers: "Shoulders back, head up, stomach in; one, two, three . . . ."

It stood in the front gallery at the Museum of Modern Art, so that I could go by to see it without even going into the building. Sometimes as I stood there peering through the glass a passerby would stop and try to see it. One guy looked at me sideways and then asked, "What is it, a wasp?" Like Mama Younger and her droopy geranium, there were days when I needed to see "Large Soft Fan." It seemed, as Mama said, to express me. It stood about twelve feet high, maybe ten, and it was one of those old black fans that used to turn slowly back and forth in your grandmother's parlor like someone listening to a conversation and turning from speaker to speaker, or like someone watching a slow ping pong game. "Large Soft Fan" drooped. Its black plastic blades and the guard around them seemed to need fanning, and "Large Soft Fan," despite its size and what it obviously was, seemed about to collapse at any moment. It had a great long power cord, as big around as a fire hose, and at the end a plug as big as a fireplug. But it wasn't plugged in, and there was about the whole thing a great helplessness. It was beautiful.

Cleopas and his friend were simply going home, but by that Easter evening they found themselves back in Jerusalem, and who knows where they went from there. Luke's story suggests the birth of the church, and we are aware already of the power that will be poured out at Pentecost. The meal which they share in Emmaus that evening is for us—whatever it was for Luke—a eucharist. And we have difficulty thinking that it was not so for Luke: the restraint of the account, the evening hour, and the familiar language—"He took bread and blessed and broke it, and gave it to them." Luke does not let us forget that this is God's doing. These people had lost heart and were speaking of their hopes in the past tense. Easter breaks in upon them, as Bornkamm sees:

> The men and women who encounter the risen Christ in the Easter stories have come to an end of their wisdom. They are alarmed and disturbed by his death, mourners wandering about the grave of their Lord in their helpless love, and trying like the women at the grave with pitiable means to stay the process and odour of corruption, disciples huddled fearfully together like animals in a thunderstorm. So it is, too, with the two disciples on the way to Emmaus on the evening of Easter day; their last hopes, too, are destroyed. One would have to turn all the Easter stories upside down, if one wanted to present them in the words of Faust: "They are celebrating the resurrection of the Lord, for they themselves are resurrected."[2]

They are, in fact, more like "Large Soft Fan" until they are *overtaken* with Easter's joy, fed and cheered at the Lord's hand. And when that happens, everything becomes possible.

2. Günther Bornkamm, *Jesus of Nazareth* (New York: Harper & Bros., 1960), p. 184.

The Second Sunday of Easter

Lutheran	*Roman Catholic*	*Episcopal*	*Pres./UCC/Chr.*	*Methodist/COCU*
Acts 4:32-35	Acts 4:32-35	Acts 4:32-35	Acts 4:32-35	Acts 4:32-37
1 John 5:1-6	1 John 5:1-6	1 John 5:1-6	1 John 5:1-6	1 John 5:1-6
John 20:19-31	John 20:19-31	John 20:19-31	Matt. 28:11-20	John 20:19-31

EXEGESIS

First Lesson: Acts 4:32-35. This lesson follows easily on the heels of the Gospel for Easter Evening. The community of witnesses, whom God is transforming to life and through whom he is transforming the whole world, has now encountered sharp opposition and persecution. Will such events turn it aside from "the way"? Luke is sure that left to its own power and wisdom it would indeed be turned aside (5:38 f.). But God creates the community of his witnesses in the invincible and closely linked events of his raising Jesus from the dead and of his sending his Spirit upon the church.

Regarding the former, note carefully the opening sentences of Peter's speech in Acts 3:12 ff., particularly 3:13. When was it that God "glorified his servant Jesus"? Luke probably intends a double reference (a) to God's deed of raising Jesus from the dead, (b) to the present dimension of that deed in God's making Peter a witness through whom he (God) raises to health the lame beggar. Jesus' resurrection is both back there and here now.

Regarding the latter, Luke mentions the Holy Spirit's filling the community not only at Pentecost (2:4), but also here in the midst of persecution (4:31). It is, then, *both* in the contemporary power of Jesus' resurrection *and* in the renewed coming of the Spirit that the witnesses act and speak with joy and without fear.

Some of the inner-community dimensions of this picture are now given in the paragraph which forms the lesson. In fact, the dual character of the community's source—the resurrection of Jesus of Nazareth, and the sending of the Spirit—is reflected as a literary problem in the paragraph. Commentators have long puzzled over v. 33. It seems to interrupt a well-structured report about a pattern of communal sharing brought about by the coming of the Spirit. Clearly, however, Luke did not see it as an interruption, but rather as a link. The miracles which God powerfully effects on the public scene (4:33a) by glorifying the risen Jesus *in* the testimony of his witnesses find their inner-community counterpart in a miraculous economic sharing to which the young church is led by the Spirit (4:31-32; cf. 2:44). This sharing—certainly not "an unsuccessful experiment in communism"; note the juxtaposition of 4:33b and 34a: God's grace leads to the sharing, so that it is not "man's deed"—is effected both by holding property in common (v. 32) and by some persons (note 12:12) selling property to raise money for the needy. Luke is probably consciously aware that in these deeds God fulfills his promise of Deut. 15:4, for the LXX of that verse is essentially reproduced in Acts 4:34a.

Second Lesson: 1 John 5:1-6. It may be well to read this text backwards as well as forwards. The author of 1 John had to do contest with gnostics who denied the reality of Jesus' death, an error into which we may ourselves easily slip in a post-Easter euphoria. By the words of v. 6 the author wants to make clear that the cross was not merely a door through which the heavenly redeemer passed momentarily. He really *died*. Nor does the resurrection obliterate the cross. It is the Jesus who really died who is the risen Son of God.

Moving back, we can see that while the author's gnostic opponents divorce from one another (a) questions of belief and (b) issues of everyday life in community, the author perceives an inextricable connection between Christology and community ethics. His opponents, the gnostics (2:19), deny that the earthly Jesus is the heavenly Christ, *and* they haughtily look only to their own interests (4:20). In the author's view by contrast, to affirm that the Son of God is none other than Jesus the crucified one (in 5:1 the word Jesus receives the emphasis) is to die to "the world" of self-interest and pride (2:15-17) and to live in the practical love of the brothers and sisters (5:1 ff.). If one is offended by the fact that the author speaks of love *within* the community, he may want carefully to consider the import of 5:1b. Pondering one's own experience in family life (also in re-reading John Steinbeck's *East of Eden*), one must realize that to say that every child who loves the parent loves also the siblings is in fact to speak of a miracle which is to be observed and experienced only in the *family of God* where God effects a birth that overcomes the world of self-interest and hate (5:4). The author is well aware of the inherent integrity of the God-Neighbor-Self triangle as he says of the miracle of human love: "We love, *because* he first loved us." Just as self-interest and hate spring precisely from disobedience vis a vis God ("I shall set up on my own"), so brother/sister love springs from obedience (faith) to God who grants to such active faith the victory over evil in the life of everyday love.

Gospel: John 20:19-31. It is instructive to compare the original ending of John's Gospel (chap. 21 is probably an appendix, an important one to be sure, from a later hand) with the ending of Luke commented on above (Easter Evening) and below (Easter III). For making such comparisons, use, if possible, a parallel of the four Gospels. In the section of John 20 under perview the evangelist seems to have employed (1) a piece of old tradition, that of Jesus' appearance to the disciples in Jerusalem (vv. 19-23), which is also reflected in Luke 24:36-43 (cf. Mark 16:14). He follows this piece (2) with a two-paragraph story of his own composition designed to dramatize the emergence of doubt among Christians of his own day in the late first century (vv. 24-29) and (3) with the conclusion to his Gospel (vv. 30-31).

In the traditional piece (1) Jesus utters three sayings, all of which have essential counterparts in Luke: (a) John 20:21; Luke 24:48. (b) John 20:22; Luke 24:49; Acts 2:4; (c) John 20:23; Luke 24:47 (cf. Matt. 16:19 and 18:18). Yet the fourth evangelist has heard the sayings in his own setting, as is particularly evident in the case of the first two. (a) Luke hears the risen Lord tell his disciples that they are "witnesses of these things"; John (v. 21) hears words about the disciples' being "sent" by one who in this Gospel so often refers to himself as having been sent by the Father. (b) Luke hears the risen Lord promise later to send the Spirit; John (v. 22) hears him utter words awesome beyond measure, as, in the moment, he breathes the Spirit upon them (cf. the five Paraclete sayings in chaps. 14-16 and the motif of Jesus' ascension in chap. 17). We shall return to these sayings in a moment.

Searching for the fourth evangelist's major intentions in our text, one may recall that the tradition of a Jerusalem appearance was worded, in at least one form, in order to combat the threat of docetism (see Luke 24:39b and 43). This threat seems to be of no concern to John. He can calmly portray a body of marvelous powers, able to pass through closed doors, while elsewhere he speaks explicitly of perceivable parts of a tangible body. He is interested not in the nature of the body, but rather in the identity of the risen Lord with the man of Nazareth. Yet even this is not his major concern.

That concern emerges, rather, in the remarkably bold reshaping of the traditional sayings behind vv. 21 and 22, and in the linking of those boldly reshaped sayings to the paragraphs about Thomas. It is precisely this linking which should help us answer the old question whether the utterance of v. 21 refers only to the eleven (ten?) or to all Christians. If John's concern in the Thomas story centers in the emergence in his own time of debilitating doubt within the Christian circle, he will scarcely be interested in reshaping the saying behind v. 21 in a way which refers only to the eleven. Thus, the sayings of vv. 21 and 22 are so deeply awesome precisely because in them John hears the risen Lord (a) send every Christian into the world (15:18-27) *just as* the Father sent him into the world, (b) breathe into *every* Christian the Holy Spirit, the Paraclete.

In order to sense the *full* import of these twin utterances one must turn back to the farewell discourses (13:31-17:26) which are informed by many concerns, one of which is the fact that, with his ascension to the Father, Jesus is leaving his disciples behind in a hostile and menacing world. (He explicitly does not ask the Father to take them out of the world, 17:15.) Is it any wonder that the disciples are anxious (14:1)? Consider the words of Jesus in 17:11 f.:

> And now I am no longer in the world . . . While I was with them, I kept them in thy name . . .

The question is, Who will keep them now?

And, as if to make this question completely unbearable, the Lord proceeds, not only to leave his followers in the world, but in fact to send them into the world (17:18). In the face of these developments the disciples will not only be assailed by anxiety but also plagued by doubt.

Now, return to the Lord's utterances in 20:21 f. There are two *gifts*! The sending of the disciples into the world *just as* the Father sent Jesus Christ into the world and the immediate breathing onto the disciples of *the Spirit*. Is the Christian *left alone* in alien territory? Hardly. He is actively *sent* at the authority of the Father, and he is *given the Spirit* who is Jesus' "double" (14:26; 16:13 f.). As Thomas soon learns, the immediacy of this sending and the immediacy of this Spirit leave no room for insulating factors which breed fear and doubt. He who sends the disciples also gives the Spirit who is the *praesentia Christi*. Hence the climactic, face-to-face confession: "My Lord and my God."

HOMILETICAL INTERPRETATION

The trumpet which celebrates the church's new life in the resurrection plays a triplet, three inseparable yet distinct notes: Jesus is present among his disciples; they have everything in common; fear is overcome and the Holy Spirit is present in power. The living Lord is present with God's gathered, sharing people, and the victory he has won over the powers of death is celebrated by the cripple who walks and the people who are together, first behind closed doors and then to the ends of the earth. Though the last two lines limp for putting the wrong foot first, and peter out into a mere "something," the quatrain holds:

> The ground of all celebration
> is a circle of people
> who believe in one another
> and in something together.[1]

Acts 4:32-35. Could we live together without the cash nexus around which society coheres? How do we answer Eliot's question:

> When the Stranger says: "What is the meaning of this city?
> Do you huddle close together because you love each other?"
> What will you answer? "We all dwell together
> To make money from each other"? or "This is a community"?[2]

Isn't our status in society directly related to what we own? Would we have any community *or* identity without property lines? The communes which have sprung up in recent years have, at least, roused in us feelings of ambivalence. We cannot readily see how such a community could stay together, and we wonder if we wouldn't lose our identity in an environment like Walden II. Who would we be if we put everything we have in one pot?

An American traveling in New Zealand was warned by a European New Zealander, a *pakeha*: "The Maori people are shiftless and have no ambi-

1. Ross Snyder, *Contemporary Celebration* (New York and Nashville: Abingdon, 1971), p. 36.

2. T. S. Eliot, "Choruses from 'The Rock,' " *The Complete Poems and Plays* (New York: Harcourt, Brace and Co., 1952), p. 103.

tion, and you ought not to judge our country by them." What the traveler found, after living among the Maori for a few months, was that these polynesian New Zealanders had a different set of values from the *pakehas* in both New Zealand and America. The Maori person values, above all, talking and playing and eating with family and friends. A Maori father likes nothing better than to stay home all day telling stories to his children. A Maori's status is not determined by how much property he has, but by how well he is related to family and community. The quality of life in the community determines the Maori's attitude toward money (and the work that gets it), rather than the reverse.

The early church is bound together in the joy of the risen Lord, in the power of the Spirit, and so they share everything. That is the sequence: "And all who believed were together and had all things in common . . . ." (Acts 2:44). This is the community of teaching *and* fellowship, breaking of bread *and* prayers, daily worship *and* laying it on the line for people in need. In a community like that, it doesn't even occur to someone to say, "That's mine." Isolation from the community, as Ananias and Sapphira learn, is the way of death (cf. Acts 5).

Notice how it is put: ". . . no one said that any of the things that he possessed was his own, but they had everything in common." Doesn't that offend the works righteousness by which we lay heavy demands on people without supporting them in a nourishing community? Edith Wharton, in her novel *Ethan Frome*, paints a picture of Starkfield, the wintry gray town in Puritan New England which demands hard work and duty and even self-sacrifice of Ethan but offers him no real sustenance for living up to its law. Starkfield is all demand and no grace; it is Sinclair Lewis's unsatisfying society which demands that Babbitt, at all cost to himself and the humanity of those around him, be a "success" on *its* terms. Babbitt lives in our Starkfield, does he not?

But we see in the early church a group of people who have found a new kind of status. They move beyond a mere jockeying for position or the grudging admonition to "pay your own way" and "carry your own weight." This is not the petty economy of "If you don't work you don't eat" or the dues-paying club where status is for sale. This is the utter generosity of people who have found a new set of values. The community itself is a gift, God's gracious creation in Jesus Christ, and it is received, valued, and shared as such. What's yours is mine and what's mine is yours because what we have together is more valuable than anything I could have apart from this community. With healing and joy breaking out among them, these Christians got their priorities straight.

1 John 5:1-6. We could, of course, press the idea of community to the point of equating salvation with "togetherness." Life in the church too easily becomes, as Nels Ferré once suggested, living under an umbrella of mutual congratulation, intellectual coziness, and pot luck suppers which does not so much overcome the world as fend it off. The preacher in the *New Yorker* cartoon stands in a contemporary pulpit proclaiming "I'm OK and you're OK," and his enthusiastic congregation answers, "Amen, brother, you're OK and we're OK." That is not the picture we get from the author of 1 John.

It is a real, unavoidable world in which everything is *not* OK, and the writer holds our noses to that. The world is in the power of the "evil one" (5:19), and it is the kind of world that actually put to death the very life and light of God (cf. 1:1 ff.). No more than Jesus escaped real suffering and death at the hands of the world can we expect to live like disembodied spirits in a docetic church. This church that prays daily in celebration of Jesus' victory and rejoices in the Spirit is still *in* the world.

How do we overcome the world? More characteristically the writer would answer with what Frederick Buechner calls "consonants" rather than a blatant vowel (cf. *The Alphabet of Grace*). The writer would tell us to "have fellowship," "walk in the light," "love one another," "do right." But here it is "our faith," words which seem to flash like a neon sign with a blinking arrow pointing toward *us*. In fact, however, the writer holds together the victory of faith—"Who is it that overcomes the world but he who believes that Jesus is the Son of God"—with more homely words: "We know that we have passed out of death into life, because we love the brethren." The writer does not allow any separation between "our faith" and "loving the brethren," as if one were a noun which we have and the other something we do. Even God's commandments are both gift *to* us and demand *upon* us, as Jesus Christ is both Savior and Lord, the Spirit both impetus and power, our being together—kind, tenderhearted, forgiving one another—inseparable from the gift *and* command of forgiveness.

John 20:19-31. Here are the disciples in shuttered seclusion on the evening of that day. And here is the bold confession, "My Lord and my God." In so brief a story we follow the trajectory of faith, from fear to joy, from doubt to confession, from retreat to witness, from asking a sign to bowing down.

Here is the embryonic church, huddled between hoping and not daring to hope. Mary Magdalene has brought the news: "I have seen the Lord." But who can believe it? They have not seen him, and a knock at the door would heighten their fears more than raise their hopes. But can we doubt that hope is there, that they would be gathered at all were not the first movement toward faith already afoot, the first blush of believing already on them? There is no knock at the door, but Jesus comes and stands among them, shows them his wounds, speaks peace, and tells them, in so many words, to unlock the doors: "As the Father has sent me, even so I send you." The wounded healer, the crucified king, gives them freedom and with it a mission to make freedom mean something. The stone is rolled away, the doors are open. The power they need will be theirs as they receive the Holy Spirit, and the authority promised to Peter the Rock is promised this little band: "If you forgive the sins of any, they are forgiven . . . ." (cf. Matt. 16:19). But how can they receive such peace and power on the third day after they have seen that vulnerable flesh on the cross and their hopes sealed in the tomb? Jesus stands among them, showing them his hands and side, speaking peace and power, sending them out. Is there any sight they could see, any experience they could go through, which cannot be accommodated by the suffering, death, and resurrection of the one who has been their friend and teacher and is now their Lord and Savior? Will not the story of the cross be adequate to the ends of the earth and the end of time so that the mission on which they are sent is provided for by the very message which they are sent to tell? "Take up the cross and follow me" is both final succour and ultimate demand.

Eight days later when they are gathered in the same house with the doors shut—but here there is no mention of their being afraid—Jesus stands among them speaking peace.[1] He speaks at once to faith and doubt, to the Thomas that is in them all and in us all. "Peace be with you," Jesus says, and he invites Thomas not only to see but to touch with his hands: "Do not be faithless but believing." And Thomas, who tradition says went all the way to India from that room, speaks for them all, for the whole church: "My Lord and my God." In the world they all had, as Jesus said, tribulation. But before they left the room, the world had in fact, in them and among them, been overcome.

The Third Sunday of Easter

Lutheran	*Roman Catholic*	*Episcopal*	*Pres./UCC/Chr.*	*Methodist/COCU*
Acts 3:13-15, 17-19	Acts 3:13-15, 17-19	Acts 3:13-15, 17-19	Acts 3:13-15, 17-19	Acts 3:13-15, 17-19
1 John 1:1-2:2	1 John 2:1-5a	1 John 1:3-2:5a	1 John 2:1-6	1 John 2:1-6
Luke 24:36-49	Luke 24:35-48	Luke 24:35-48	Luke 24:36-49	Luke 24:35-49

EXEGESIS

First Lesson: Acts 3:13-15, 17-19. The Book of Acts—is it surprising?—contains its own supply of apostolic miracle stories. It also presents several times a brief encapsulation of what Luke understands to be the core of apostolic preaching about Jesus. And finally, Acts presents, as is well known, several rather finely developed "speeches" of some length. Our text is one of the passages in which these three literary forms are brought together.

(1) The miracle story presents the basic outline expected: I. A Hopeless Situation (3:2); II. The Miracle (3:6 f.). III. Confirmation (3:8-10). Prior to Luke's editing, the story probably concerned only Peter and the lame man ("with John" looks secondary in v. 4; Peter does all of the talking and acting; Luke is concerned to have two witnesses appear before the Sanhedrin in 4:5 ff., especially 4:20). There is also little doubt

1. See the hymn, "They Cast Their Nets in Galilee," *Pilgrim Hymnal*, p. 340.

that in its traditional form the story placed emphasis on the healing act "in the name" of Jesus Christ. For Luke, as for the traditioner from whose hand the story came to Luke, the "name" of Christ is one of the loci in which the risen Lord exercises his gracious power on earth. It is not the name of Luke's culture but rather of his Lord.

(2) The brief encapsulation of "the Jesus Kerygma" may be seen when one compares 3:13b-15 with 2:23-24, 32; 4:10; 5:30-32; and 13:29-31. It seems to have three major elements: (a) The Jewish authorities *delivered* Jesus up, (b) but God reversed that line of action by *raising* him from the dead, and (c) by bringing into existence faithful *witnesses.* Luke never presents this encapsulated kerygma by itself. He always ties it to a setting by means of at least two of its elements. The word "raised" in v. 15 points back to the word "glorified" in v. 13, which, in turn, points back to the miracle.

(3) Peter's speech (vv. 12-26) contains "the Jesus Kerygma," but also goes far beyond it. Compare Acts 2:14 ff.; 4:8 ff.; 5:29 ff.; 13:16 ff.

Luke shows both great literary skill and theological potency in the combining (and composing) of these three elements. Regarding the possibility of a double entendre in the word "glorified" (v. 13), see the second paragraph of the exegesis for Acts 4:32-35 (Easter II). Beyond that one notices that Luke extends the miracle story and the brief kerygma into a speech which indicates that it is *God's grace* and nothing else which *calls man to repentance* (v. 26). There is no presupposition which the lame man must fulfill before he can be healed. God simply chooses to glorify his servant Jesus by bringing people to health. Do you believe that God's grace precedes your faith? Believing that is what repentance is all about.

Second Lesson: 1 John 1:1–2:2 (or 2:6?). Re-read the exegesis of John 20:19-31 (Easter II), especially the comments about the farewell discourses and their importance for understanding John 20:21 f. Now, come to 1 John. We are listening to a preacher who has faced the threat of being left as an orphan (John 14:18), and who, in the face of that threat, has been allowed to hear (note the primacy of this biblical verb), to see, and even to touch the life which was from the beginning. Where and How?

Part of the answer is given by the literary probability that our author is a preacher who has lived with the fourth Gospel so closely for so long that its message has permeated his manner of speaking as well as his theology. Beyond this it is clear that the "major character" of that Gospel has himself spoken to this preacher through its pages, and in those moments the preacher has heard and seen and touched the one who says so majestically,

> I am the resurrection and the life; he who believes in me, though he die, yet shall he live, and whoever lives and believes in me shall never die. (John 11:25 f.)

Our preacher has also heard this one say:

> I am the light of the world; he who follows me will not walk in darkness, but will have the light of life. (John 8:12)

The one who is life did not remain in a distant sphere, but rather came to be manifest and to be heard, seen, touched. The preacher has heard, seen, touched. He stands, therefore, on solid ground.

But one notices also that all of these verbs of perception are plural. It is *we* who have heard and seen and touched. While one can be sure that 1 John was written by an individual (2:1, etc.), he does not understand his essential existence to be individual in character. He has heard the one who speaks in the pages of the (fourth) Gospel *as* that Gospel is read in the Christian fellowship. It is not in a lonely trance, therefore, but in the fellowship that he and his brothers and sisters perceive.

Perceive whom and perceive what? In our author's setting the second question is as necessary as the first. For he lives in the real world in contact with people who use a word dear to his heart—fellowship—while showing in their daily lives a pride and self-assurance which annuls the gift of life. They are not irreligious people. Exactly the opposite. Indeed one of their favorite sayings has an unexceptionable ring to it:

> We have fellowship with him (1 John 1:6).

There is a tip-off, however, in another of their sayings:

> We have fellowship with him and are without sin (1 John 1:6, 8).

And while they are very lively people who believe they have discovered their own essential congeniality with the eternal light, perhaps intending to refer to nothing less than John 8:12 (above) as they say

> We are in the light (2:9),

they straightway prove that they are still in the darkness by showing no love for the brother.

Our author makes no compromise with such people (2:19); yet neither is he mesmerized into a preoccupation with them. His concern is for the building up of the fellowship of Christians who are in every way forgiven sinners, and whose love for one another springs precisely from their knowledge that in their daily confession of their sins they are bound to the Lord who faithfully forgives both them and every other member of the human family (2:2).

Gospel: Luke 24:36-49. The Gospel for today consists literarily of a pre-Lucan tradition regarding Jesus' post-resurrection appearance in Jerusalem (vv. 36-43) and of a penultimate paragraph in which Luke is able to communicate in powerfully dramatic form major dimensions of the story of Jesus and his new people (vv. 44-49). For literary analysis see the exegesis on Luke 24:13-49 for Easter Evening.

It is not difficult to see that Luke has allowed the traditional piece to set the scene for the crucial pronouncement of the risen Lord which follows it. In its pre-Lucan use the traditional piece clearly had some anti-docetic dimensions (note vv. 39 and 43). In the technical sense these seem of no great concern to Luke. He is intent, rather, on the motif of *empowered continuity*. The path followed by the one who healed the sick and who taught the way of the Lord did not find its end in the cross. On the contrary, that same one now comes to his frightened, erstwhile followers and puts their feet on the extension of that path. How?

In the first instance by showing them the path in a book! In its long journey (Acts 1:8) the church will need again and again to search the scriptures for guidance (a lamp to the path); and this need makes necessary, in turn, a true hermeneutic. Hence Luke's concern with the hermeneutical question.

Notice, however, that this question is not merely a matter of scribal acuity. It involves making the scriptures an "open book" in a radically new manner. In fact Luke uses the verb "to open" in remarkably instructive ways: twice in the Emmaus story and once in the Lord's crucial pronouncement. The reader first learns that the Emmaus stranger is suddenly recognized because in the moment of his breaking the bread the *eyes* of the two disciples *were opened* (v. 31; cf. v. 16). Next, after the Lord's withdrawal, these two disciples ponder the fact that their hearts had burned within them as he talked with them along the road and as he *opened the scriptures* to them (v. 32). Finally, these two motifs are brought together, as the risen Lord *opens* the disciples' *minds* to understand the *scriptures* (v. 45).

Of what, exactly, does this "new hermeneutic" consist? In the main, of two points. (1) The scriptures bear witness to Jesus as the Christ (v. 27); the hermeneutic is Christocentric. (2) The specificity of this scriptural witness is communicated by three infinitives (in Greek) which demonstrate precisely the empowered continuity: It is written in scripture for the Christ *to suffer*, for him *to rise* from the dead, and for repentance and forgiveness of sins *to be preached* in his name to all nations, beginning from Jerusalem (vv. 46 f.). The risen Lord gives his church a radically renewed vision of scripture which will guide their feet on the path already traveled by him. This is a great gift (cf. 2 Cor. 3:16-18).

Yet there is more. The disciples will walk in "the way," not only under the guidance of scripture, but also in the power of the Spirit. It is to Pentecost that the Lord points in v. 49. The Spirit will come and will clothe the young church—the scriptural interpreters—with the power of God himself.

HOMILETICAL INTERPRETATION

Easter's victory occurs among people who are lame, guilty, afraid, sometimes joyful, often disappointed. Perhaps "victory" is too triumphal: the people we know, both in and out of the Bible, will limp and cower and feel the pangs of guilt on many a fine spring morning. The texts for today point not so much to the *fait accompli*, though there is that, as to a continuing relationship and obedience to Jesus Christ. Jesus did not speak so much of final victory as of the peace that the Spirit would constantly give. The fearful women of that first Easter, the doubting Thomas, the sequestered disciples: they will all continue to fear and doubt and hide as we do. But the word we hear today witnesses to God's continual overcoming of sin and death. Isn't that just the word we need to hear two Sundays removed from Easter Day? Is there anybody here who is lame, if not from birth, then periodically? "But if we should sin. . . ." Does that hit us? And do we still walk the road to Emmaus, wondering?

Acts 3:13-15, 17-19. ". . . the God of our fathers has glorified his servant Jesus." The language points to the days of his flesh, which led some to glorify God and some to reject Jesus. What obtuseness and willful blindness could have failed to see the glory that was there all along, so manifest in his very humanity? Is it not the same alienated dullness which keeps us from seeing our own true situation as God's children? How could it happen that people with ordinary human feelings could have preferred a murderer and given over to death the Author of Life? Peter does not hesitate to point the finger: "You delivered up . . . you denied . . . you asked for a murderer." And there is the word of compassion, or at least of realism: "And now brethren, I know that you acted in ignorance, as did also your rulers." But there is no hope in that, in making excuses. Peter's brief gives way to gospel.

"But God. . . ." It is God who is at work in all of it: your denial, Pilate's cowardice, Jesus' suffering. God is using all of this, life as you have warped and spoiled and misused it, to glorify his servant Jesus. He has turned the whole affair to his own purpose. Beyond all fixing of blame, Peter witnesses: You have in your ignorance chosen death when you put Jesus to death; you have not been true to even the most elemental human instincts of decency and worth. But God has, nevertheless, raised him, and all who follow him, to life. Peter does not invite argument. What matters is that God has used the shame to show forth the servant's glory and that we are called now to read in his suffering the marks of our own true status. In Jesus God opens our eyes to what is. He causes us to walk and he turns our walking to dancing.

Peter's message lives in its context, as if the sermon were being acted out as he preaches it. The man lame from birth is raised at the hand of Peter in the name of Jesus. Jesus is raised, and people who see the meaning of that are turned away from death to life. And it is all of God: it is the goodness of God *which is always there* that leads us to repentance (cf. Rom. 2:4). Thomas Oden has said:

> The purpose of proclamation is that of calling man to an awareness of the reality of the situation in which he already exists, the reality of God's occurring love; not to introduce God to his world, as if he were not already there, but to introduce man to himself as one who is always already claimed by God.[1]

So much is God already there claiming us as his own that even in the ignominious death of an innocent man his love can shine through. There we are illumined, our eyes are opened, and we see and dance out what has been there all along:

1. Unpublished paper, Drew University, 1973.

Hear him, ye deaf; his praise ye dumb,
Your loosened tongues employ;
Ye blind, behold your Savior come;
And leap, ye lame, for joy.

1 John 1:1–2:6. The writer describes a community of grace which we have hardly known. He confesses at the same time the human condition and God's grace, and he sees the church as the people among whom we confess: "But God shows his love for us in that while we were yet sinners Christ died for us" (Rom. 5:8). In the community of grace it is possible, beyond all pretense and clamoring for status, to face up to our condition: "If we say that we have no sin, we deceive ourselves. . . ." How is it possible for people to face themselves and to know each other and make it together? We sometimes achieve it in the family. Home is, as Frost said, "the place where when you go there they have to take you in." But even families are not always at home with each other. How can any other group hold together intimately without the lubrication of the cocktail party? How does a community of *sinners* cohere?

The author points to something that has happened: We can't forget what we have seen with our eyes and touched with our hands—the word of life. And we can't help telling you what we have seen and heard. In fact, we tell you this so that you may come with us out of darkness into the clear daylight. We can look at ourselves and each other with wide open eyes because God has opened our eyes to himself. We can have life together because God has said Yes to us, and that Yes is spoken in the face of every No that we can say to ourselves and to each other. There is no longer any need to avert our eyes from the worst that we can do or the worst that could be done to us. God has pulled the stinger.

We need not pretend, lie, or even try to be "somebody." This community is built upon something prior. Where else but in the presence of God who in Christ forgives and renews could people say out loud together:

> We confess to you, God of the oppressed and oppressors, and to you our brothers and sisters, that we ourselves are not only oppressed but oppressors as well. We are black, red, yellow, brown, white; male, female; western, eastern; Asian, African, American, European; schooled, unschooled; lower class, middle class, upper class; suburban, rural, inner city; married, unmarried, divorced; heterosexual, homosexual; Protestant, Catholic, agnostic, atheist. We confess that knowingly and unconsciously we have been accomplices to imperialism, sexism, racism, consumerism, and ageism.[2]

The holy catholic church. I believe in it. I've even seen it in the flesh once or twice. I believe in God the Father . . . Jesus Christ . . . Holy Spirit . . . the forgiveness of sins.

You sit across the kitchen table from that person who has been saying no to himself for years, perhaps for all the years he has had. You are grateful for coffee that gives you something to do, or else you might speak too quickly and say what is on your mind: "O come off it. Why can't you

2. Unpublished liturgy of the Fisherfolk Community, Camden, N.J., 1975.

admit what you are and where you've been and be yourself?" But you don't say the words. Would you be heard if you could get it out: "Why don't you slow down and let the Lord love you?" or "Why not give up trying to be a nice guy and let the Lord make something good out of you?" But it all remains unspoken. What kind of environment would make it possible to speak the truth in love and to be heard? How, and where, can you let people know that God is saying Yes all the time and that even the No which they are feeling and fixating on is part of his Yes?

The writer imagines a community where that takes place, where we admit to one another how it is with us and praise God together, where redemption and worship occur east of Eden. Such a community is possible when we remember the message of Easter, that it is *God's* doing. It is when we praise God together that we are able to be together. "Where there is no temple there shall be no homes. . . ."[3] Whether we worship in folding chairs in the round or continue to sit in pews side by side, our life together is our life facing the altar in praise of him who knows us and forgives us and binds us. It is in such a community that we experience *at the same time* the two things we need all our lives: to be held responsible and to be, finally and beyond all striving, held.

Luke 24:36-49. Where do we go from here? What does it all mean, the suffering and death of Jesus, my suffering and that of people I know? Is there anything to be salvaged from wrecked hopes? What could possibly put together the pieces of the puzzling occurrences which preoccupy the two travelers to Emmaus?

Luke frames their conversation with two stories which focus on Jesus their friend and teacher. In fact, the focus is on his body. The insistent sensuality of the Christian story borders on being embarrassing. It begins with a red baby born among the redolent earthiness of a stable and moves toward the naked body on the cross, tenderly taken down by Joseph and wrapped in linen to await the women with their spices and ointments. Small wonder that artists have painted Christianity's every scene: the body is always there.

But Luke's frame is to give both context and emphasis to his central image: two puzzled companions who are moved from seeming dismay to discipleship. What happened to send them running back from Emmaus to Jerusalem?

In Grünewald's triptych, the long finger of John the Baptist points to the vulnerable body on the cross. In his other hand John holds an open book: "Behold the lamb of God!" In Luke's story, Jesus points from the book to himself, and the experience of that Friday becomes comprehensible to Cleopas and his companion. Experience is raised to the level of meaning: Jesus crucified becomes the lamb slain from the foundation of the world and through the long history of Israel, and he becomes the lamb

3. T. S. Eliot, "Choruses from 'The Rock,' " *The Complete Poems and Plays* (New York: Harcourt, Brace and Co., 1952), p. 103.

worthy to receive blessing and honor, dominion and power. The death of Jesus is caught up in the larger story of God's redemption, and in that new understanding the past transforms the present and opens toward the future.

We limp and sin and wonder, and it can all sink down to life that is out of joint with nothing connected to anything else. But God opens our eyes, in the name of Jesus, to see who he is, and our story is caught up in God's story, and we are given a mission, courage, and joy.

> Rejoice in the Lord always; again I will say, Rejoice. O Thou, Thou who didst call us this morning out of sleep and death. I come, we all of us come, down through the litter and letters of the day. On broken legs. Sweet Christ, forgive and mend. Of thy finally unspeakable grace, grant to each in his own dark room valor and an unnatural virtue. Amen.[4]

The Fourth Sunday of Easter

Lutheran	*Roman Catholic*	*Episcopal*	*Pres./UCC/Chr.*	*Methodist/COCU*
Acts 4:8-12	Acts 4:8-12	Acts 4:5, 7-12	Acts 4:8-12	Acts 4:5-12
1 John 3:1-2	1 John 3:1-2	1 John 3:1-8	1 John 3:1-3	1 John 3:1-8
John 10:11-18	John 10:11-18	John 10:11-16	John 10:11-18	John 10:11-18

EXEGESIS

First Lesson: Acts 4:8-12. This is the third of Peter's post-Pentecost speeches and the first of two which he makes while standing before the Sanhedrin (5:29-32 is the other). We need to be clear about the setting, and then about the structure of the speech itself.

The setting is specified by the note in 4:2 that the Sadducees arrest Peter and John because the latter affirm in Jesus the resurrection of the dead. If one emphasizes Luke's expression, "the resurrection of the dead," the note seems to make good sense: The Sadducees, who vigorously deny this doctrine, arrest the apostles for proclaiming it. On second thought, one will see, however, that this syllogism makes no sense at all. Were this doctrine itself the point at issue, the Sadducees would need to arrest all Pharisees, and, indeed, hosts of the general populace as well. What causes the rub is the connection between *Jesus* and the resurrection and especially the connection in terms of *current events*, such as the healing of the lame man. Pharisees who affirm the doctrine of the general and future resurrection are quite tolerable. Ignorant men (4:13), on the other hand, who are instrumental in healing people in the "name" of a condemned criminal whose resurrection they affirm already to have been accomplished by God—such men are unbearable. They must be silenced. Hence they are called to account.

4. Frederick Buechner, *The Alphabet of Grace* (New York: Seabury, 1969), p. 112.

As Luke pens such scenes it is clear that he recalls Jesus' prediction:

> [Before the cosmic terrors of the end time] they will lay their hands on you and persecute you, delivering you up to the synagogues and prisons . . . . This will be a time for you to bear testimony . . . . I will give you a mouth and wisdom, which none of your adversaries will be able to withstand or contradict. (Luke 21:12 ff.; cf. Matt. 10:17 ff.)

Thus, while the formal outlines of the situation call for a scene in which prisoners speak in their own defense, the true dimensions of the situation are reflected in the fact that they do not speak in their own defense, but rather bear witness to God's contemporary deeds. For to these deeds those who propose to sit in judgment are themselves subject, whether they realize it or not.

The setting is thus not at all what the Sadducees imagine it to be. Rather than being just another day in the history of jurisprudence, it is a stage along "the way" which leads victoriously from Jerusalem to the ends of the earth.

As to the structure of the speech itself, it is in the main similar to the others: (1) A comment about the situation itself (4:8-9; cf. 3:12 and 2:15) is followed by (2) two-thirds of the "Jesus Kerygma" (cf. Easter III): (a) You crucified Jesus of Nazareth, (b) God reversed that line of action by raising him from the dead, and by (3) a clear indication of how this kerygma is related to the situation. In the present speech the relating of kerygma and situation is accomplished by focusing attention on Jesus' *name* (cf. 3:6, 16).

The ancient orientation to the name of a person and especially of a god is in play here. A name is not a mere convenience; it is rather something which participates in the personhood of the one to whom it belongs, and it is therefore not really separable from him. If he is truly named, he is at least partially present in terms of his power. Hence a wise man does not name a god lightly.

Once again we see that the road did not end in the cross. To be sure, the Sanhedrin might logically think that to be so. It had passed its judgment (Luke 22:66 ff.), and Jesus had been crucified at Pilate's hands. Yet here are these Christians standing with a healed man and saying that God gave him his health (salvation) when they demanded in the name of Jesus that he walk. In what they say about Jesus' name, they clearly affirm that Jesus is alive and active. Exegetes ponder whether the pronoun in the last clause of v. 10 should be translated "him" (so RSV), referring to Jesus, or "it," referring to Jesus' name. Perhaps the grammatical ambiguity should be accepted as an unintended index of the presence of Jesus' power in his name.

The final verse has occasioned a large literature over the centuries. Luke's intention is quite clear. *All* lines of history are flowing together into the emerging great church, in which one therefore recognizes that Jesus Christ is *the* Lord (Note Acts 14:15-17; 17:22-31). One may find it profitable to imagine a conversation between Luke and Franz Rosenzweig (see N. N. Glatzer, *Franz Rosenzweig* [1972], pp. 341-348).

Second Lesson: 1 John 3:1-2 (3:1-3). Re-reading the comments on the texts from 1 John for Easter II and Easter III will provide needed background for the present text.

The context is set partly by the note of 3:7, the danger of church members being deceived and led astray. Who might deceive them, and how might he lead them astray?

The answers are clearly enough given in 3:8 ff. The author takes for granted not only the existence of the devil, but also his active participation in human affairs. The latter is reflected in the author's affirmation that, like God himself, the devil has children. That is to say, he does not merely exist "somewhere"; on the contrary, he is active and effective in human society through children of his own. What do they look like? They might be quite attractive and highly religious people, through whom one could be led astray, but in every case they are revealed to be his children by one clear mark of distinction: Like Cain they manifest the "original sin" of the devil—they do not love their brothers.

Over against this picture the author places that of the children of God portrayed in our text. We can be sure that he has read and pondered many times John 1:12 f., verses which retain overtones of their connection with baptism. In that event the person becomes a child of God, not through any effort of his own or through any power of his biological parents, but by God's own graceful action. The thought is very old (cf. Hos. 11:1 ff.). In Jewish thought of the Hellenistic age God's action is (a) affirmed as a future hope and (b) introduced into a dualistic framework, as in the Qumran writings and in Jubilees (1:24 f.) and in the present passage: there are sons of light and sons of darkness, children of God and children of the devil. But we must understand that this does not necessarily bring with it a deterministic motif. Our author simply observes two distinct patterns of life, and wishes his readers not to be deceived into thinking there really is no difference between the two.

What guards members of the fellowship from such deception is their knowledge that God has graciously made them his children, thus both enabling (4:19) and commanding (3:11) them to love one another. All of this—and more—is gathered up in the remarkable practice followed in the author's community of calling God "*The* Father" (twice in the synoptics; 75 times in the Johannine Gospel and 14 times in the Epistles).

Whereas the author of Jubilees (see above) expected the gift in the future age, our author affirms it for the present. Correspondingly, awesome as it is already to be children of God, there is more, a very powerful "not yet." It is not powerful as a result of the painting of colorful and detailed apocalyptic pictures. On the contrary, all is focused on the Father himself and hence on the promise that seeing him—recall both John 1:12 f. and John 1:18—will bring about a marvelous transformation in us. We *shall* become similar to God!

(There is a knotty exegetical problem in v. 2; the statement just made stands on the election of one interpretative alternative. Following the words "we know," the author has employed a passive verb whose subject is difficult to fix. Should we translate, "We know that when he is revealed . . .," or should we render it, "We know that when what we shall be is revealed"? Schnackenburg makes a strong case for the latter. The result is that 3:12 speaks about God and his children and does not mention Christ. However, the other alternative is not at all to be excluded as a possibility, and, following it, one would read the text as a reference to Christ's parousia and to the children's becoming similar to him when they see him. In either case the vision is sharply focused on the Godhead, and the promise is that our present experience of God's remarkable love in making us his children will be followed by the yet more remarkable event of our becoming similar to him. [We do not meet here the thought of man's ultimate divinization. That would be a gnostic motif foreign to the author.])

Gospel: John 10:11-18. Raymond Brown in his commentary on the Gospel according to John (pp. 388 f.) has given the structure of John 10. The first five verses present two parables: (1) vv. 1-3a: There is a proper way to approach the sheep, through the gate; (2) vv. 3b-5: There is *the* shepherd, and there are alternative shepherds. Following these parables, vv. 7-10 explain the gate parable, and vv. 11-16 (to which vv. 17-18 are attached) explain the parable of the shepherd.

The latter explanation falls into two parts: (a) vv. 11-13 explain the shepherd parable by introducing new characters and new motifs. There are wolves; their coming spells danger; in that context a hired hand saves his own neck; the model shepherd, on the other hand, lays down even his own life for the sheep. It is difficult to be sure who the hired hands are, but the relationship with John 9 will suggest that those who proved themselves blind to Jesus' presence as the Light of the World by handling so roughly the formerly blind man are here thought of as hired hands who have no genuine concern for the people entrusted to their care.

(b) Vv. 14-16 (17-18) offer a second interpretation, which follows the parable itself more closely by emphasizing the shepherd's intimate knowledge of the sheep. It is a typical and impressive Johannine note to heighten the intimacy of the relationship between Jesus and his own by placing it as a typology (". . . just as . . .") with the relationship between the Father and the Son (v. 15a)!

Two further motifs call for comment. (1) The entire passage is framed by two affirmations of Jesus about his own death (vv. 11 and 18). The second of these is polemically formulated. Perhaps there are persons in the evangelist's setting who interpret Jesus' death as an execution: the responsible judges ruled that Jesus' life was to be taken, and so it was. "Not at all," replies John. Jesus is himself the one in complete authority, who lays down his life in order to re-take it!

(2) The motif of v. 16 has played a large role (along with John 17) in the modern ecumenical movement. We cannot be certain of its import for John, but many interpreters take it to be a reference to the Gentile mission. If so, it is one more witness to the early Christian conviction that

the worldwide mission is a component of Jesus' death/resurrection itself (cf. John 12:31).

HOMILETICAL INTERPRETATION

The power of the texts for today is dialectical. New life is set alongside the old, the children of God against the "world," the good shepherd over the hired sheepsitter. The collage is light and darkness, the contrasts extreme.

We meet these NT witnesses as preachers whose message can hardly be bridled to one metaphor or held back from hyperbole. The bigger the truth, the wilder the metaphor. As we hear—or better, overhear—the early church celebrating the new life, there is no need to try to make everything "fit"; that can end in gutting one text to suit it to another. The gospel cannot be homogenized, and we would be suspicious if it all turned out to be as neat as a three-point sermon. We rejoice in these disparate witnesses who reveal their humanity as they cast about for words to say the one thing they are sure of: Whereas we were in darkness, lame, hungry, and lost, now we are made whole. Overhearing them is like hearing the children's song:

> Sometimes my voice is as small as a mouse,
> And sometimes my voice is as big as a house.
> But it's all right, it's all right,
> Because the song is always beautiful.

Acts 4:8-12. The force of a sentence is at its end: "and by him this man is standing before you well." Peter is speaking before theological skeptics and political conservatives. He might have debated with them the possibility of resurrection or he might have attacked their alliance with Rome. But he simply points to the man, past forty, crippled from birth, who stands before the assembled political and ecclesiastical powers of Jerusalem. We can only dimly picture the scene: two "uneducated, common men" and a middle-aged man whose great distinction is that he can walk, before the old high priest, his family, and associates. Where does Peter get his words? From the message he has heard? A report of resurrection? From the rapidly growing, supportive community of Christians? From John, who simply stands there with him? From the lame man? What is the connection between Peter's bold speeches and the tradition that the risen Lord appeared first to him? However we account for Peter's words, Luke says that he was "filled with the Holy Spirit." He finds his voice: "This is the stone which was rejected by the builders, but which has become the head of the corner. And there is salvation in no one else. . . ." It is a very big voice indeed! The humble poor believe and the forgotten crippled dance in the temple, and the new life they know in the crucified and glorified servant is of another sort altogether than might be won by protecting one's worldly position or kowtowing to Rome. No name, not even Caesar's, could do what the "name" of Jesus has done for these three men standing here. The redeeming story accomplishes what the how-to pragmatism of political and technological manipulation could never achieve. These are people "made whole"—it is as close as we can come in English to salvation of body and spirit—metaphors themselves of the unlikely cornerstone. Peter, who has at last become a rock, would have understood the metaphor well.

1 John 3:1-2. "Beloved, we are God's children now." Here and now, just as we are, in the flesh and too often of the flesh, we are God's little family. Pretty cozy. You could get the picture here of a clutch of people gathered around a groaning table, the draperies drawn and the warm glow of congeniality fending off the hostile world outside. Or you could imagine a beleaguered cadre locked in an upstairs room, fear bordering on paranoia, or at the very least, exclusiveness. John gives us the makings of either scenario. The passage is surrounded by "antichrists," "the children of the devil," and the "world." The godless world is shut out of the little circle because it does not know God as we do.

We could set the stage that way, and there is reason to do so. John writes in the midst of contending religious cults and threatening heresy, and he is concerned for purity. He turns inward toward the community, and his central concern is that those who follow Jesus should abide in Christ and love one another in the church. But he keeps his feet. This is no mere "I'm OK, you're OK, aren't we great!" Far from it. John begins where he ends, with the unaccountable love of God.

"See what love the Father has given us. . . ." That is the only justification for calling ourselves his children, and if we have any success in loving each other and doing right, it is his doing as he works among us. And we can't even say what will become of us, how we will turn out, as if "every day in every way" we were "getting better and better." That is not John's thrust at all. We abide in him, confident that the same love which, beyond all our doing, keeps us from sin (cf. 3:9) today will shape our life together in the future. For the present and for the future, for what we are and are becoming, it is being in Christ that matters. This is not the coziness of a self-assured group living above sin, despising the "world." It is more like being grateful that you can see and walk, or feeling deep down that sense of belonging and being known when parents' love turns sharing meals and a house into a home that frees and heals. It is that awareness of the Father, and the goodness of his creation and his grace in Jesus Christ, which leads us to hope that we may become like him. The awareness of love which leads to love, holds us together and gives us the future.

John 10:11-18. The contrasts between the new life and the old are stark. "I am the bread of life." This is the true bread, as health-giving as the manna come down from heaven and as dependent upon the Father's goodness. This bread is the opposite of that which does not satisfy (cf. Isa. 55), of that "light" bread which is white and soft but does not nourish us. Anyone who eats this bread will not be hungry; this is soul food such as you can get at the H&H Cafe down in Macon, Georgia, where the menu is written out in pencil and there *is* no decor and they've never heard of MSG and you can have six vegetables and boiled beef and cornbread. Two dollars flat! And the next time you spend twenty dollars for two you remember Isaiah: "Why do you spend your money for that which does not satisfy . . .?"

"I am the light of the world," shining in the darkness "I am the resurrection and the life," shouted into the very teeth of death. "I am the *good* shepherd." We understand that, especially in a society like ours, where so much is superficially attractive, where the very economy is built on making it so. There is so much to tantalize the palate, titillate the imagination, and appeal to the insatiable need for the new, or at least the novel. Who can really feed the people? Where is life, illumination, joy, peace? Who can fend off the wolves, win the real battles, stay with us through the night and prepare the banquet table at noon? Is there another name that we can trust? Who are the hirelings, who the good shepherd, here in our town, on our main street? (Cf. Jer. 23:1-4.)

This is one of those texts that has such a voice of its own that we find preaching it like following a big anthem, or like making a sermon of Tillich's our own. We would just as soon leave such a text to itself, or to stained glass windows or Handel. We wish that we were musicians or painters, or that we could dance it out like lambs at play in the fields of the Lord.

Some would say that the difficulty of preaching on the passage is its pastoral setting. "I am the good shepherd. I know my own and my own know me. . . ." What can it mean to me? I am not sure I want to be a sheep! I have hardly *seen* a good sized flock of sheep in my life, and they had never been near a wolf. And as for shepherds, I've seen a few pictures in *National Geographic* and some in Christmas pageants. Maybe I would do better to find another metaphor: "I am the fool-proof computer: you are instantly retrievable," or "Social Security has my number, I shall not want."

But that doesn't quite do it. The heart of the passage is inseparable from the *kind* of knowledge which the shepherd has of the sheep: "I know my own and my own know me, as the Father knows me and I know the Father." When I hear the words, "I am the good shepherd," I feel that I am known where I really live. In this city, where "sheep" mean someone easily taken in, or out on this farm where sheep are managed by fences and fleeced by machinery, I know what it means, "I am the good shepherd." I feel that I am known where I myself am the wolf and the hireling, and just because of that I am the sheep in need of the shepherd who knows me and lays down his life for me. There is a place at the heart of my life—where I am afraid and run away and bare my teeth, and where I am a lamb—to which I am always trying to invite other people. But most cannot know me there at all, and some would manipulate and handle me in that place. Even my father and mother, my spouse and children, my best friend, cannot often stay with me there when the wolves come. But "thou makest me to lie down in green pastures, thou leadest me beside still waters, thou preparest a table . . ., thou anointest my head with oil."

The ironies are many. The good shepherd, himself the lamb of God, saves the sheep but cannot save himself. His rod is both grace and judgment, his kingly sceptre a shepherd's crook. He knows and guards his own flock, but the whole world is his fold. His kingdom embraces the world but is not of the world and is finally as close to me as his own relationship to the Father, as near at hand as his words: "I am the good shepherd." And I wish I were the Hallelujah Chorus to answer, "Worthy is the lamb that was slain. . . ."

The Fifth Sunday of Easter

Lutheran	*Roman Catholic*	*Episcopal*	*Pres./UCC/Chr.*	*Methodist/COCU*
Acts 9:26-31	Acts 9:26-31	Acts 9:26-31	Acts 9:26-31	Acts 9:26-31
1 John 3:18-24	1 John 3:18-24	1 John 3:18-24	1 John 3:18-24	1 John 3:18-24
John 15:1-8	John 15:1-8	John 15:1-11	John 15:1-8	John 15:1-8

EXEGESIS

First Lesson: Acts 9:26-31. We may grasp some aspects of Luke's work as a Christian historian by comparing two paragraphs in Acts 9 with the pertinent data in Paul's own letters.

Acts 9:19b-25 // 2 Cor. 11:32 f.

In this paragraph Luke paints two pictures of Paul in Damascus immediately after the latter's conversion. He seems to fill out the first picture merely from the fact of the striking contrast between Paul's activities before and after his conversion. For the second, he clearly had a tradition about a dramatic escape from Damascus, for Paul also speaks of the event in 2 Corinthians. Comparing the two texts enables one to see that an event which was probably fundamentally political has been portrayed by Luke as exclusively religious.

From Galatians we learn that immediately after his conversion in Damascus Paul went to Nabatea (1:17). Luke does not mention this fact for a simple reason. He is writing church history; Paul did not succeed in establishing any churches in Nabatea, or perhaps did not try to; hence no tradition came to Luke about Christian activity in Nabatea. What may very well have transpired there is that Paul came afoul of the king, Aretas. In any case, Paul returned from Nabatea to Damascus (1:17).

In doing so, he did not entirely remove himself from the grasp of Aretas, since the latter maintained a governor or a charge d'affaires in Damascus. Through this minister Aretas attempted to arrest (not kill) Paul, but the Christian brethren enabled him to escape by lowering him in a basket through an opening in the city wall (2 Cor. 11:32 f.).

If we assume that Luke received a tradition similar to the report Paul himself gives—and the wordings are in some regards quite close—we may note how he shapes and changes it. Luke is not interested in Paul's "political" relations with the Nabatean king and his minister in Damascus. His canvas at this point is concentrated on the "religious" tensions between representatives of Judaism and those of "the way," and he portrays these tensions as growing rapidly. Hence he presents a picture in which Paul's adversaries are not Nabatean soldiers, but rather "the Jews," and their intention is not to arrest Paul, but rather to kill him.

Acts 9:26-30 // Gal. 1:18-24.

The comparison just made will help us here. Again it is clear that Luke had at his disposal a piece of tradition: a notice of some sort about a trip made by Paul from Damascus to Jerusalem. If it was similar to the report Paul gives in Gal. 1:18 ff., we may once more see Luke's editing.

In the Galatian letter Paul speaks of going from Damascus to Jerusalem three years after his conversion. It was a brief visit of two weeks, and his contacts were severely limited. He conversed only with Peter and James. He says nothing about having preached while there.

We cannot be sure, of course, that Luke received exactly this picture in his traditions about Paul, but if he did, his handling of it is striking. He first introduces the dramatic note that the Jerusalem Christians were afraid of Paul, not believing him to be a Christian. This is probably a note of Luke's own making, since it is quite unlikely that after three years (Gal. 1:18; cf. Luke's own "when many days had passed," Acts 9:23) news of the extraordinary genuineness of Paul's conversion would not have traveled from Damascus to Jerusalem. The note is designed to catch the reader's interest.

Next, Luke says that after Barnabas showed him to be "kosher," Paul went about in Jerusalem, so to speak, arm in arm with the church leaders, preaching and entering into disputation. We can be sure Paul would have been amazed at this picture, and perhaps much more than amazed (cf. Gal. 1:20). For Luke, however, it is a natural portrait. He certainly did not intend to distort, but rather to show what he takes to be essential: Paul's mission—to the ends of the earth—grew out of and therefore developed in continuity with that of the Jerusalem church. Luke's interest is shown quite clearly, in fact, in the summary of Acts 9:31. It is remarkably ecclesiological. Whether through Peter, Stephen, Philip, or Paul, it is God who is building up and multiplying his one church.

Second Lesson: 1 John 3:18-24. Again we see the inextricable connection which the author weaves between "theology" and "ethics." God's commandment (3:23) is that we believe in the name of his Son Jesus Christ (developed in 4:1-6) *and* that we love one another (developed in 4:7 ff.) However, the new note, as compared with texts in 1 John already commented upon, is struck in 3:19-21, verses which occasioned much attention from the church fathers and which may speak in a remarkable way in our own context.

The heart stands here, of course, for the human conscience. Two possibilities are open to it. It can condemn the ego (v. 20), or it can abstain from condemning the ego (v. 21). In the author's world, as in our own, people put much store in the power of the conscience precisely for this reason. Does the author endorse the guidance of the conscience, perhaps "Christianizing" it in the process? Not at all. He clearly considers the conscience to be anything but a reliable guide. Of course it is there, and it cannot be ignored; but neither is it to be followed.

Does he then throw his readers into the chartless labyrinth of complete relativism? Hardly. For the Christian the conscience is no reliable guide precisely because God has invaded his very being with his word of grace which is also his commandment. When the author says that God is greater than our heart-conscience, he has in mind a quite specific situation: that of the Christian who is living in loving relationships within a Christian community and who is plagued by an inner accuser. He is to say to the inner accuser, "God is greater than you are. Be gone!" Obviously this does not mean that the Christian has become autonomous. Far from it. What has happened is that the quite unreliable conscience has been replaced by the direct invasion of the gracious and demanding Father who sets the person in that community in which the Father's commandment to love the brother is in fact kept. Perfectly kept? Of course not. But in instances in which it is not kept, one does not fall again under the tyranny of the conscience. One remains in the presence of God, with the advocate whom God has provided: Jesus Christ the righteous (1:9; 2:1). It is because of the gifts of Christ and the Spirit in the community of Christian love (3:23, 24) that we can know in daily experience that God is greater than our condemning conscience.

Gospel: John 15:1-8. The structure of John 15:1-17 is similar to that of 10:1-18 analysed for Easter IV: a parable drawn from pastoral or agricultural life is provided with interpretation. In both instances we find what we might call a fine interweaving of Christology and ecclesiology.

This interweaving is handled somewhat differently in 15:1-6 and in 15:7-17, so that the present reading tastes of both. In vv. 1-6 third person language dominates the imagery, without, to be sure, obliterating the use of the second person, and the relationship between Christ and his church is represented in a timeless parable. In vv. 7-17 the second person is consistently used, and we find numerous themes proper to the Last Supper. There is a resulting movement of thought from the supra-temporal unity of vine and branches to the specificity of this unity in the gospel story itself, and this movement is crucial in keeping the rich imagery of vv. 1-6 from becoming an end in itself. More on that in the comments for Easter VI.

Having heeded the warning not to read vv. 1-6 as the whole story, we may allow them their role. They constitute what the Jews call a *mashal*, a broad parabolic form from which some small degree of allegorical over tones should not be excluded: "I am the (real) vine" (vv. 1 and 5), "My

Father is the gardener" (v. 1); "You are the branches" (v. 5). Through the entire picture runs the dualistic choice of remaining or not remaining in Jesus, and the whole of life turns on it. There is no ecclesiology without the massive Christology which stands always at the center of John's picture. Given this massive Christology, the present reading, divided as it is, may be taken as a commentary on the meaning of a community of disciples which is fruitful in the world because of its thoroughly christological nature (v. 8).

HOMILETICAL INTERPRETATION

One way of viewing today's texts is to set them in the much-traveled terrain between pietism and activism. We are uncomfortable in either camp: pietism seems incapable of validating itself, and activism is all too easily prone to self-confirmation. What is the relationship between the vision and the mission? Between contemplation and getting with it, between Blake's "braces" and "relaxes"? Is it true that the end of the religious life is to glorify God and enjoy him forever, and if so, what is the profile of the person in the act of glorifying God? The readings for today do not give us the kind of answer that we can put in our pocket like a two-dollar bill. Instead, they force us in this Eastertide to think again about the source of our confidence *and* of our activity.

Acts 9:26-31. The most obvious fact about Paul is the apostle's validation of his ministry by his experience on the Damascus Road. You don't even have to press him to get him to push his chair back and say, "Well, I am doing this and telling you this story because once upon a time when I was traveling to Damascus. . . ." That is, of course, what all of us ultimately have to do in giving account of who we are and what we are doing: "Something happened to *me* once. . . ." The emphasis which Paul wishes to give to the story which lies behind his message and mission is at least part of the reason for the differences between his own account of his conversion and ministry (cf. Galatians 1) and that of Luke. What Paul wishes to stress is that the gospel he preaches is not a second-hand "man's gospel": "For I did not receive it from man, nor was I taught it, but it came through a revelation of Jesus Christ" (Gal. 1:12). And even in Luke's account, when Barnabas brings Paul before the apostles, he emphasizes the experience on the road, how Paul had "seen the Lord, who spoke to him" as a way of accounting for his reported boldness in preaching to the people of Damascus.

The way in which the question of pietism and/or activism presents itself to us would have made little sense to the early church. The very impetus for all they did was the continuing, vivid experience of the risen Lord. All of Paul's preaching and traveling, his disputing and apologetics, rose from an experience which was his own and which was constantly renewed in both his victories and in deprivation. We can only imagine the importance to his active, sometimes whirlwind ministry of the years in "Arabia," a period of withdrawal which is foreshadowed immediately after his experience on the road as he waits, blinded and immobilized, for a brother to come. How do we, as we give account of what we are doing in the name of Christ in this town here and now, relate our doing to being in Christ? What is the role of the Spirit and of our brothers and sisters in leading us from our private experience toward useful work in the community? Doesn't Luke suggest throughout Acts an inseparable relationship between worship/fellowship on the one hand and mission to the world on the other? Whether we take Paul's account, in which he lays emphasis upon the kind of experience which we usually identify with pietism, or Luke's, who is eager to tie Paul to the community, any effort to separate what we do from what God has done for us in Christ fails.

1 John 3:18-24. To do God's will: what is that? What is expected of us? What sense can we make of the language of *abiding*? The word probably suggests to us something like passive dependence. What would our lives look like if we were really abiding in God? Does that suggest a great deal of church going, or private prayer, or elevated moods, like always being on cloud nine?

Abiding in God is certainly not a passive hanging around in holy precincts. John makes that clear: "All who keep his commandments abide in him and he in them." And keeping his commandments is not just a matter of pious talk or ecclesiastical good manners: ."Little children, let us not love in word or speech but in deed and in truth." The pastoral counsel of this letter could not be more straightforward: to be in Christ is to *do* something, to demonstrate by our style of life that we are being led by the Spirit.

At the same time, we do *abide* in him. This passage seems tailor-made for the American experience in which we are constantly oscillating from one extreme to the other. But here, doing and being are not allowed to fly apart. We are called to do the deed, but we are, for all our doing, "little children." Demand is laid on us at the same moment that grace meets us. At every moment, we abide in God, even when we fail to match deed with word. Even when we condemn ourselves—when we do not live up to the most elemental responsibilities of being God's people—we abide in his grace: "God is greater than our hearts." So marching for peace and sitting down for justice and boycotting for equality, we are justified by grace, not in the doing itself. And even when we pray, we must ask the spirit to intercede for us.

There is in Graham Greene's novel, *The Power and the Glory*, that ne'er-do-well, drunken priest who, despite himself, is able to be an instrument of grace in a disrupted society. His very ineptness points to the power of the Spirit which uses him, and there is about him an integrity of purpose which Greene sets over against the dour proper missionaries whose religion seems as external to their persons as a pair of ill-fitting shoes. The priest abides, hangs on for dear life, and is able, as a "wounded healer," to minister.

It is the sense of dependence, the knowledge that no day and no deed is well undertaken which is not begun in Christ, which is life in the Spirit. To *abide* in him is to believe and to do, to speak and to act, to pray and to preach, to keep house, push pencils, and make pies. It is the same Spirit which causes all these moments to shine with new meaning. In exalted moments and common tasks, "by this we know that he abides in us, by the Spirit which he has given us." Is this a unique relationship? Is there any other in which we know such ultimate demand—"all who keep his commandments abide in him"—and such final acceptance: "God is greater than our hearts, and he knows everything"? Even the analogies of marriage and old friendships seem not quite adequate to express that kind of being at home.

John 15:1-8. By what analogy can we see more clearly the organic connection between act and being? "Abiding" and "bearing fruit" are one and the same where horticulture is concerned, whether you take it from "The Fantastics"—"plant a turnip, get a turnip"—or from the Gospels: "By their fruits you will know them." To be a grape vine *is* to bear grapes, and we assume disease or a trick when a vine which appears to be grape does not manifest grapeness in clusters of fruit. To be in Christ, to live in the fellowship of the Counsellor, is to bear predictable fruit.

When we hear the words, "bear fruit," do we think first of measurable production, of quantifiable results, such as we tally up at the end of a month or a year? What is this fruit? Do we understand the metaphor if we picture the vinedresser counting out tangible contributions to the church, or success in enlisting new church members, or our self-consciously undertaken good works? No one interpreting the passage for practical, pragmatic Americans would want to disparage those good works. On the other hand, our inclination toward the philosophy of success—"Nothing succeeds like success"—is at once our virtue and our vice. The first fruit of the spirit is love for one another. That is what issues in good works and evangelism, the sort of tangible deeds which we often equate with Christian fruitfulness.

Paul's catalogue of the fruits of the Spirit occurs in the context of pastoral counsel on Christian *freedom*. Legalism and works-righteousness "sever" us from Christ (Gal. 5:4), and the signs of being cut off from him are abusive acts toward our own bodies and toward other people. On the other hand, "the fruit of the Spirit is love, joy, peace, patience, goodness, faithfulness, gentleness, self control. . . ." (Gal. 5:22). Being in Christ produces the very attitudes which are essential to living with other people! Can we say that abiding in Christ *is* being in community? Is it Christ who makes true community possible? Do we agree with T. S. Eliot?

> There is no life that is not in community,
> And no community not lived in praise of God.[1]

1. T. S. Eliot, "Choruses from 'The Rock,' " *The Complete Poems and Plays* (New York: Harcourt, Brace and Co., 1952), p. 101.

"I am the *true* vine." We can have confidence in the fruit which comes from that vine, even hope that God may be glorified in that fruit (cf. Matt. 5:16). How many of our own motives can we trust so confidently? How many crusades and ideologies, faddish movements and pop causes last long enough to give us *hope*? Herbert Butterfield, at the end of *Christianity and History*, tells us:

> We can do worse than remember a principle which both gives us a firm Rock and leaves us the maximum elasticity for our minds: the principle: Hold to Christ, and for the rest be totally uncommitted.[2]

The more we are involved in the immediate problems which plague our society and the world, the more we could ponder those words and what it is to abide in Christ the true vine. What can both nourish and motivate us, set us free and give us security? Apart from Christ, how many of our causes will end up at the city dump as smoldering garbage?

Walter Rauschenbusch was the foremost figure in the American social gospel movement. He labored to better the lot of working people, campaigned for political candidates, and worked for such mundane social improvements as sandboxes for New York's poor children. At the same time, he preached warm, simple, biblical sermons to his small congregation in Hell's Kitchen on New York's West Side, and his own personal religious life was as deeply devout as that of his Lutheran and Baptist forebears. He spoke of prayer as stepping aside and entering through "a little postern gate," to a place where he was renewed and guided. Few have achieved Rauschenbusch's integration of action and devotion. The Gospel for today promises us such wholeness: to be in Christ the true vine is having and sharing new life.

The Sixth Sunday of Easter

Lutheran	*Roman Catholic*	*Episcopal*	*Pres./UCC/Chr.*	*Methodist/COCU*
Acts 10:34-48	Acts 10:25-26, 34-35, 44-48	Acts 11:5a, 11-18	Acts 10:34-48	Acts 11:5a, 11-18
1 John 4:1-11	1 John 4:7-10	1 John 4:17-21	1 John 4:1-7	1 John 4:1-11
John 15:9-17	John 15:9-17	John 15:9-17	John 15:9-17	John 15:9-17

EXEGESIS

First Lesson: Acts 10:34-48. Acts 10 is often referred to as "the first conversion of a Gentile: Cornelius." That is quite correct, but only part of the picture. It also narrates the conversion of Peter, and that is where the major accent lies. Peter and his companions in the Jerusalem church—all Jews (10:45)—assume that God's new people constitute a circle within the larger circle of Israel. They are in for a surprise. God leads them into a new world-view.

2. Herbert Butterfield, *Christianity & History* (London: Fontana, 1957), p. 189.

First, by a dream Peter learns not to call any food cleansed by God (10:14 f.) or any man created by God (10:28) common or unclean. The Kosher rules do not dictate the contours of the church. Second, there is the matter of the Spirit. Jews who are Christians may learn to have some degree of association with Gentiles (vv. 28 f.), but surely the gift of God's Spirit, which empowers the church, is limited to Israel. But no, this wall also comes tumbling down. For even as Peter speaks, God breaks the "rules," by sending the Holy Spirit on *all* who are listening (v. 44). We may now notice how crucial to the speech are the little words "all" and "every":

> v. 35 . . . in *every* nation . . .
> v. 36 . . . He is Lord of *all* . . .
> v. 43 . . . *every* one who believes in him . . .

As is always the case in Acts, the speech and its context are thus carefully inter-related.

The speech is remarkable on several counts. It gives the fullest outline of Jesus' ministry outside the Gospels. This would seem appropriate in a speech made to Gentiles in Caesarea, and so it is. But one may also note the literary artistry of Luke, who really addresses this speech to the readers of his two volumes. For it is these readers, and not Cornelius, who by having read the first of his volumes, already know the story of Jesus (vv. 36 ff.). And it is they, whether they be Jews or Gentiles, who are now to be converted as Peter was, so that they learn that God does not turn over his lordship to any set of national or racial rules as such, but rather intends the Spirit-empowered mission for *all* people. This is not a matter of a good "liberal" feeling. It is a matter of God's choice and of his action (15:7).

Second Lesson: 1 John 4:1-11. This reading comprises two sections which are distinguishable, yet closely interrelated.

(1) *4:1-6.* One may re-read the comments on 1 John 3:1-2 for Easter IV. The dualistic framework is, of course, maintained in the present passage, and specifically vis a vis a crucial matter in early Christianity—cf. 1 Cor. 12:10—the discerning of the spirits. The author is convinced that his readers live in a world in which, even as regards the church, there are numerous "options." In the face of these options one will need criteria for discernment, and the author unashamedly finds such criteria in what we call dogmatics. The matter of confession is not something which can as well fall this way as that. It is *the* question of life.

In the author's context a major option was offered by gnostic prophets (4:1) who had the "right" slogans (see Easter III) and who—surely in an "intelligent" manner—identified the savior as the essential Christ, a figure who temporarily appeared in the guise of a man called Jesus. It is not difficult to see how such people might have developed their thought on the basis of *some* elements in the Johannine Gospel. They certainly understand themselves to be Christians.

To the author this situation makes necessary a distinction between "orthodoxy" and "heresy," and he makes it on the basis of the confession that Jesus Christ came *in the flesh*. The Christology which finds its center in Jesus of Nazareth as God's Son is here distinguishing itself from an otherworldly retreat into metaphysics alone.

(2) *4:7-11.* As is clear from earlier passages, the "heresy" inevitably reveals itself not only christologically, but also in everyday relationships (4:8, 20). Hence, once again, the emphasis on love of brother.

The modern reader may find it strange, finally, that the love of brothers is the content of God's *commandment* and hence of *exhortation* (4:7). It is a result of the development of romantic love in Western culture that we speak of "falling in love," being "struck by lightning," etc. By contrast the author thinks of love as being subject to the will, once one knows that God has loved him first.

Gospel: John 15:9-17. One sees the extraordinary care expended on the composition. As Raymond Brown has shown in his commentary on the Gospel according to John (p. 667), we find one of the numerous cases in John of a chiastic pattern enclosed by vv. 7 and 17: If . . . my *words* remain in you, *ask* for whatever you want . . .; the Father will give you whatever you *ask* . . .; this I *command* you.

Several motifs call for special comment:

First, as was remarked in the exegesis for the preceding passage (Easter V), the paragraph is strongly marked by the interweaving of Christology and ecclesiology. We may see this interweaving in a kind of diagram:

Just as the Father loved me,
also I have loved you:
  Remain in my love
  (This is the place–*topos*–for the Johannine community.)
How does the community abide in Christ's love?
  By keeping his commandments,
  just as he kept the Father's commandments, abiding in his love.
What are these commandments?
  Only one: love one another,
  just as I have loved you.
Because I have elected you, you are my friends.

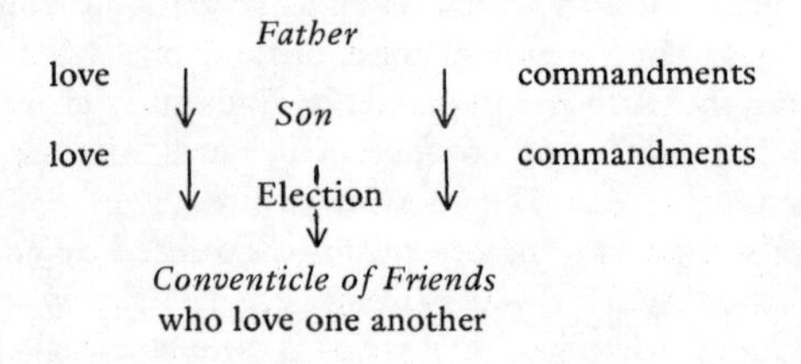

To put it boldly, the verb "remain in," which is so central to the parable of the vine and its branches, is now explicated in such a way as to suggest that the corporeality of the community with Christ is in some regards comparable to the relationship Christ has to the Father.

Second, the paragraph very nearly begins and ends with a second expression taken from the parable: "to bear fruit." What does it mean? A strong clue is given in v. 16. As is appropriate to the parable itself, bearing fruit is not something a branch decides to do of itself. In terms of v. 16, a person is a fruitful branch not because he has chosen Christ, but because Christ has elected him to the "apostolic" ministry, has laid on him the single-minded commandment to love his brothers, and has given him himself and the fellowship as the place of his abode. To bear fruit is thus not a matter of an individual's deed as such; it is rather a matter of the life of love in the community.

Only *in* the community? The question may justly be posed, not least because of the paragraph which follows (15:18 ff.). The picture of the vine and its branches is surely a portrait of what we might call conventicle piety. Outside is "the world," which hates the fellowship (15:18, 19, 23), and persecutes it (15:20), even to the point of inflicting death on some of its members (16:2). We are surely in touch here with some of the marks of the actual experiences of John's community, experiences which have reinforced its feeling of estrangement from a largely hostile environment.

Yet it is equally clear that the world is the object of God's love (3:16), and that Christ has "other sheep" (10:16). Hence the conventicle piety is no end in itself, but is rather the beachhead which God has established, and which he is enlarging for the sake of all men (12:32; 11:51 f.). It is for this reason that the conventicle-like fellowship is of such vital importance. In short, the joy of which v. 11 speaks is the joy of a community which has *both* a tightly-knit identity of mutual love *and* a world mission, just as the joy of Christ is had both in his immediate relationship with the Father and in his coming into the world.

HOMILETICAL INTERPRETATION

There is little in the NT to provide texts for the kind of navel-gazing which asks repeatedly: "Who am I?" Rather, the preoccupation of the early church is with questions of corporate identity and responsibility: "Who are *we* as the people of God?" and "What is expected of us?" The church whose internal conversation we overhear is marking itself off from the world of darkness, death, and hatred, to use John's categories. And the community is trying to get its feet for mission, to understand how it is related to its environment and how that relationship is shaped by the word which both breaks in dynamically and remains a fixed point. We can hardly miss the difference of emphasis in John and Acts: one turns in toward self-understanding, the other is moving out to the alien, even hostile "world." But in both, the church's identity *is* its mission: to be to all persons what Jesus Christ is to his people. Who we are tells us what we are to do, just as what has been done for us tells us who we are. That word "abide" crops up again, and it pushes us here beyond individualism and exclusivism toward the kind of community which is both living and sharing the new life. That was the first word we heard this Eastertide: Jesus who is raised in power among us is to be proclaimed to the ends of the earth.

Acts 10:34-48. "God has no favorites. . . ." Peter, a Jew, and now one of the favored leaders of the Jerusalem church, makes such an admission, and before non-Jews in the house of the god-fearer Cornelius. The very city of Caesarea, from which Rome ruled the province of Judah, should have put Peter on the defensive, reinforced him in provincial and conventional attitudes. But the opposite is true. Peter seems almost surprised at himself: "I need not tell you that a Jew is forbidden by his religion to visit or associate with a man of another race. . . ."

There is about the story a warm and simple humanity, an atmosphere in which ideology and doctrinaire exclusiveness, of whatever sort, do not thrive. Cornelius runs out to meet Peter and welcomes him with such respect that Peter protests: "I am a man like anyone else." The centurion has invited his family and friends to meet Peter, and they seem eager to listen to him. Luke paints a picture of the very situation which Peter describes: Peter preaches peace in a setting of peace. The Holy Spirit comes upon these people gathered at home, and they are filled with ecstatic joy.

What is it to be in peace—at peace with God's creation and all his creatures—and so to be able to preach peace? What prior, profound experience sets aside Peter's fears and his commitment to behavior which in another setting he would deem proper to his station? At that gathering in Cornelius's house, did Peter's preaching bring peace and joy, or was there already the atmosphere of being together *as human beings* which helped to open both preacher and people to the word? Peter had had his vision beforehand in Joppa, of the goodness of creation. And his sermon shows that he understood the gospel of the resurrection as breaking all boundaries of time, place, and status. He appreciates fully the history that God has been pleased to use: "He sent his word to the Israelites and gave the good news of peace through Jesus Christ. . . ." But the risen Christ is Lord of *all*. That is not a claim to special privilege for those who follow him, but genuine recognition of his lordship and of the fertile soil for his word, openness to his spirit, and readiness for his peace which are there by virture of our common humanity.

A course is now being given in one of our seminaries on "Story, Humanity and Preaching." How often does our preaching and witnessing fail because we withdraw, exclude, and condescend? And how far is that from this family gathering and the meeting of two men which ends in the gifts of the Spirit and baptism?

1 John 4:1-11. But Christian inclusiveness is not moral anomie or a bland permissiveness. Legalism and license are not, after all, so far apart: both are essentially indifferent to the significance of human experience, to the weight of existence. The Johannine pastoral advice is direct and does not hedge in drawing sharp lines: "But do not trust any and every spirit, my friends; test the spirits to see whether they are from God . . ." John doesn't mumble when it comes to the test he would apply: those who belong to the community can be recognized by their acknowledgment that Jesus Christ has come in the flesh. It is the *man* Jesus with whom we have to do, and John wants nothing to do with people who aren't interested in the person that the apostles have heard, seen, and handled.

John goes further: he is interested in people who can be heard, seen, and handled right now. The true community is validated, finally, by the actual quality of its life in the flesh. This is God's family, inspired by God's spirit, and such a group of people can be recognized. Is that so? Where would *we* draw the lines? Are Christians healthier? Do they make more money, or use it better, or show more taste in the houses and clothes and pleasures they buy with it? Aren't we on safer ground just to stick to creedal distinctives? Christians are people who have been baptized and believe certain things. But John marks out the community of faith not only doctrinally but according to practice: "everyone who loves."

"Lifestyle" is the common coin for it today, and John describes the Christian's style with a word that is as worn as "relevance" or "my friends." "Love" has become as insubstantial as a gnostic Christ! But the writer calls us to it, and he ties the word, the hallmark of the Christian community, to what we know of Jesus Christ in the flesh, Lord of his church. Are all who live in love his? What would that look like, living in love? The answer, of course, depends upon our paradigm for the word. John makes clear who his own model is.

John 15:9-17. The gospel echoes 1 John: "Let us love one another, for love is of God." Jesus calls his disciples to be imaginative lovers, to let appear in their own daily lives the love with which the Father loves the Son and the Son his friends. The assumption here is a modern one. You can't just go out and be a lover; you need someone to imitate. A good many high-priced magazines make money on that premise. What paradigm of loving is adequate for the church? What can save us from mere sentimentality? What could bind a group of people together so that they would really want to spend more than an hour together hiding behind pews and organ music on a Sunday morning? What could make people listen to each other? Could any model of loving overcome the prejudices of economics, sex, race, and taste?

Whatever success we have in making such a community is not merely the predictable result of our autonomous planning and action, if we follow John. The branches draw their life from the true vine: new life in the community is life in Christ. The more we mature, the more we come to understand what it is to "dwell." Beyond all mere self-reliance and playing at being God, we learn what it is like to be connected, to be at home in him and with each other. Structure becomes freedom, ties become life, law becomes grace, and joy becomes full as joy was full in the obedient Jesus.

But how often is this actually realized in a human community? How often do we manage even a one-night stand of the humble, joyful loving which we see in Jesus Christ? What would it be to *dwell* in his love together? That would be the ideal community: loyal and outgoing, kind and demanding, at home and on the move. When Josiah Royce tried to imagine such a group of people, the best model he could come up with was the ideal church. But where does it exist?

The victory of the resurrection is that this new life is always breaking forth out of death. The community is constantly being created by the reality that already exists in Jesus Christ: "You did not choose me; I chose you." All that follows depends on that prevenient decision for us: "Go and bear fruit . . . love one another." God's love is there before and after all our efforts to love other people, and ourselves, and gives us the courage to stay with ourselves and other people through an afternoon and a night, or a gray morning, when we have hurt or failed or betrayed or hidden from the people who love us and whom we love. The victory of the resurrection is that this new life is always being created again in us because the separation of person from person, of persons from themselves and God, has been overcome, finally, and we only wait and try, by stops and starts, to get our eyes open to the fact and our ears and hearts open to the people around us in whom the resurrection takes flesh today. We are seeing among us today, in people being made whole as they are called from the deserts and closets and backrooms to come and be human together, the fruition of God's deed in Jesus Christ. The signs of God's victory are the unmistakable banners of love. Where are they in your church? Who has been called in, held up, supported, confronted, healed, challenged? In your family? Who has been heard, recognized, talked with, given time? Paul Tillich writes:

> Where one is grasped by a human face as human, although one has to overcome personal distaste, or racial strangness, or national conflicts, or the differences of sex, of age, of beauty, of strength, of knowledge, and all the other innumerable causes of separation—*there* New Creation happens! . . . resurrection means the victory of the New state of things, the New Being born out of the death of the Old.[1]

Where are you celebrating the resurrection in your own life today? What is new, open, hopeful? Or if there is nothing, are you waiting, dwelling, abiding? Do you think that living with silence, failure, and loneliness could be part of abiding in Christ and showing forth his love?

1. Paul Tillich, *The New Being* (New York: Charles Scribner's Sons, 1955), pp. 23-24.

The Ascension of Our Lord

Lutheran	*Roman Catholic*	*Episcopal*	*Pres./UCC/Chr.*	*Methodist/COCU*
Acts 1:1-11	Acts 1:1-11	Acts 1:1-11	Acts 1:1-11	Acts 1:1-11
Eph. 1:16-23	Eph. 1:17-23	Eph. 1:16-23	Eph. 1:16-23	Eph. 1:16-23
Luke 24:44-53	Mark 16:15-20	Luke 24:49-53	Luke 24:44-53	Mark 16:15-20

EXEGESIS

The three Ascension texts are remarkably complementary, especially if one reads them in the order in which they were written:

Gospel: Luke 24:44-53. One may wish to review the exegetical notes on Luke 24 for Easter Evening and Easter III. The added paragraph is what calls for comment here.

As the risen Lord had broken bread with the Emmaus disciples, their eyes were opened, and he vanished out of their sight (24:31). Now, having appeared in Jerusalem, and having given the disciples a new hermeneutic and the promise of the Spirit, the Lord leads them out to Bethany and takes leave of them for the last time.

In *this* context it is an arresting note that there should be three instances of the verb "to bless" (vv. 50, 51, 53), and one mention of the word "joy" (v. 52). Taken together these are clear indices that the sorrow which wracked the hearts of the disciples as a result of the crucifixion has indeed been overcome by Jesus' resurrection; and that the anxiety which could so easily attend the risen Lord's final departure has already been vanquished by the gifts of opened eyes, a mission to carry out, and the sure promise of the Spirit to empower the mission.

Some educated readers of Luke's own day would easily think of the sorrow of Socrates' disciples upon his death. Here, by contrast, there is great joy, precisely upon the Lord's departure, for he is the victor who will shortly pour out the Spirit to guide and empower his followers. His ascension begins the mission of his church through the whole of the world.

First Lesson: Acts 1:1-11. One has to recognize, first, that the very idea of following a Gospel with a sequel, a second volume on the history of the church, was not only unheard of prior to Luke's efforts, but also almost unthinkable. From a careful reading of the other Gospels it is clear that the earliest understanding of the literary form resulted from narrating the story of Jesus in a way which included the contemporary dimensions of that story in the life and destiny of the church (see, e.g., Matthew 10). There was, in short, only one story.

Now, in Luke's hands, a new horizon appears. There is still only one story, but it unfolds in epochs which may be presented and contemplated also in their own right, and this reflects a great shift in the church's understanding of itself. We can be sure that it never occurred to any member of the highly eschatologically conscious church of the first decades to make the church an object of historical inquiry. Yet this is exactly what Luke has done. Motifs of "world-foreignness" common to the earliest communities—and continued and developed in different ways by the gnostics—are left behind in Luke's understanding of the church. Indeed, he sees the growth of the church not as a sign of the imminent end, but rather as *the key to the whole of world history*.

Several aspects of the present text make this clear. Luke is conscious of writing literature (1:1) about a movement which may be described historically and chronologically (1:8). In the first paragraph, which overlaps the penultimate paragraph of the carefully structured final chapter of his Gospel (cf. Luke 24:36-49 with Acts 1:1-8), Luke allows the disciples to speak in such a way as to place the major point in relief. They ask whether it is now the end time (1:6); and Jesus corrects them by substituting a very long—one may say linear—end time (1:8). The correction is then placed in italics by being repeated: At the ascension, the disciples gaze after their master into heaven as though that were the locale in which they themselves belonged. "No," say the two angels, "do not stand here gazing into heaven. Your task is to wait in Jerusalem for the promised Spirit, who will lead you with the gospel to the end of the *earth*."

It is not a call to mere action, of course, as constrasted with contemplation. One will not credit the angels with an exhortation to roll up one's sleeves and get to work. The correction has to do, rather, with the *scene* of *God's* action, which he will carry out, to be sure, in and through his people. Jesus' ascension means not that the sequel to his earthly life will be played out in a supraterrestrial realm, but rather precisely the opposite. He will pour out the promised Holy Spirit upon his flesh-and-blood witnesses, who will then march through the world for its healing. Luke would easily have understood John 3:16. It is the world which God is in love with, and his being in love with it is its salvation.

Second Lesson: Eph. 1:16-23. The document opens (1:1-2) in the form of a letter, yet without a clear indication of the addressees, unless, as seems unlikely, the words "in Ephesus" stood in the original text of verse one. There follows—without an exact counterpart in the letters confidently ascribed to Paul—a lengthy eulogy to God, in which the author emphasizes the comprehensive nature of God's over-arching redemptive plan, into which both he and his readers have been gracefully brought (1:3-14). For numerous reasons it appears that the document is essentially a homily written by a Jewish Christian who sees his Gentile Christian brothers to be in danger of losing vital contact with his group. The homily finds its center in the picture of the Body of Christ as encompassing believers of both Jewish and Gentile heritage. That is to say, for the author the church has itself become a large part of theology. This fact makes possible a profitable comparison of Ephesians with Acts.

Note that immediately before our passage lies a paragraph (1:11-14) which Käsemann has taught us to compare with the Cornelius story of Acts 10 (see Easter VI). One may paraphrase:

> *We Jews* who first hoped in Christ have been destined and appointed to live for the praise of the glory of him in whom also *you Gentiles* were sealed with the Holy Spirit after you had heard the word of truth . . . and had believed in him.

It is God himself who broke through the limits of the old people of God in order to include also the Gentiles (cf. 2:13 ff.). The Jewish Christian author is amazed at this; he also gives thanks for it. His thanksgiving is formally expressed in our passage, which actually consists of a brief thanksgiving (v. 16a) and a long intercessory prayer (vv. 16b-23). One senses again the Jewishness of the author when one compares this passage with the thanksgiving prayers of Qumran; just as one senses his Christian faith expressed in a kind of creed in vv. 20-23.

It is this creedal expression, of course, which makes the passage an ascension text. The author draws, no doubt, on previous formulations. Compare Phil. 2:9 ff.; 1 Pet. 3:18 ff.; and Polycarp 2:1 f. The confession has three major accents: (1) God's raising Christ from the dead, (2) his exalting him to his own right hand, and (3) his subjecting all powers under Christ's feet. The author has expanded the creed by adding a fourth element, which is designed to explain the full significance of the first three: (4) The resurrection and the ascension and the exaltation above all powers of the cosmos find their meaningful goal in the fact that God has made Christ head of the *church*, which is then specified to be both Christ's body and the fullness of Christ, who fills all in all.

The Jewish Christian author surveys what we would call the ecumenical scene, and sees that the *cosmic* lordship of Christ is effected in and through the *church*, where the dividing wall of hostility between Jews and Gentiles is broken down (2:14). It is a hermeneutical task of some proportions to try to hear the voice of this Christian brother across the years and tears of the Holocaust; and the health of the contemporary church may be to no small degree dependent on such hearing.

HOMILETICAL INTERPRETATION

With what images will *we* celebrate the elevation of Jesus to kingly power? Language strains and metaphors limp as we try to preach in the blunt way expected of us on this day at the end of Eastertide and on the verge of Pentecost. The presence of the living Lord with his people bursts the bounds of the shuttered room and reaches beyond Jerusalem to the ends of the earth and the end of the age. Time and space cannot contain what Luke and Paul have experienced in the days of Pontius Pilate and on the road to Damascus. It may be true that the cloud of glory may not be as real to us as to Luke, or even "up" so powerful an idea as it was before Mercury and Apollo became names for our technological prowess. But we, nevertheless, between Easter and Pentecost, celebrate both his absence and his presence.

Eph. 1:16-23. For the apostolic witness, the exaltation of Jesus is inseparable from the new life in Christ: "... in union with Christ Jesus ... [God] raised us up and enthroned us with him in the heavenly realms. ..." (2:6) We may be less able to handle language like that than images of ascension! The author describes a "high" that, to his mind, is the normal state of the church as it is raised up to a new life of forgiveness. We are, he says, delivered from "this present age" and from the "spiritual powers of the air" (2:2). The whole epistle reads like a hymnbook and the two themes play back and forth, both in the discrete pericope and in the overall composition of the book: You are raised up with Christ; in your new life you bring praise to him. "Praise be to the God and Father of our Lord Jesus Christ, who has bestowed on us in Christ every spiritual blessing in the heavenly realms ... in order that the glory of his gracious gift ... might redound to his praise." (1:3-5)

These twin themes are the background to the apostle's words: "Because of all this ... I give thanks ... I pray." Where people are forgiven and know it—only the *knowing* is problematical—Christ is exalted. All that God has done, in prophets and psalmist and lawgiver, has moved toward this: a group of men and women freed from guilt and fear, open to each other, grateful and liberated for the future. What better metaphor than "body" could we find? This visible people in its diversity, weakness, and humanity is as inseparable from Christ as body from spirit.

The apostle prays for those "inward eyes" which can see both the unbelievable freedom and power which people together in Christ actually have, and, at the same time, the enthronement of Jesus Christ above all merely earthly power. The writer searches for words to sing "Worthy is the lamb," and he comes out with what may appear to us quite a mundane picture: people at peace, living together in love and joy, are the transfigured body of Christ. Where, in the whole universe, is there greater praise to Christ than people at peace living together in love? There is that painting of Dali's showing Christ both crucified and exalted at the same time. This Christ looks down from his cross upon a scene of the greatest tranquility in which people quietly work and where even earth and sky seem to be transformed in each other's embrace. Where are the signs among *us* that the apostle's prayer has been answered?

> Grant, we beseech thee, Almighty God, that like as we do believe thy only begotten Son our Lord Jesus Christ to have ascended into the heavens; we may also in heart and mind thither ascend, and with him continually dwell, who liveth and reigneth with thee and the Holy Ghost, one God, world without end. Amen (Common Prayer, for Ascension)

Luke 24:44-53, Acts 1:1-11. It is not easy to see what is at hand, or to appreciate fully what we already possess. In fact, as Peter Rinkoping discovers in Frederick Buechner's *Entrance to Porlock*, we must sometimes have the best taken from us and returned as gift before we recognize it as precious. How often do we actually "see" members of our families and our closest friends when they are absent? Is it any wonder that the Ephesian writer prays that the church may have inward eyes to see the absolutely astounding wonder of the gospel which can take on such homely form?

Luke begins *Acts* by recalling his Gospel in which he had tried to tell all that Jesus did and taught. He recalls that Jesus had been with his followers for forty days between Easter Day and Pentecost. Then, in the very midst of that recital, we hear the plaintive disciples: "Lord, will you at this time restore the kingdom to Israel?" The kingdom was there, in their very life together and in the words and deeds of their Lord which were their inalienable possession, and they did not see it! How much distance do we need to see clearly? Jesus had promised his friends, as he prepared them in the upstairs room, that the Comforter would teach them all things concerning himself. Could that promise be kept only in his absence? The prophet is not without honor, except among people who know him *too* well. Had the kingdom been a snake, it would have bitten them many times before they saw it.

The response to their question is both understatement and the patience of a man who knows that he has done all that he can do but who knows also that God's kingdom is already coming: "It is not for you to know. . . . But you shall receive power. . . . " Jesus has made his witness to the kingdom—it is there in what he has said and done—and now they are to be witnesses. They do not bring the kingdom, as if it were indeed a governmental and geographical estate over which a king might reign from David's throne. They are *witnesses* to the kingdom as it has already appeared in Jesus. It is true that this kingdom will be ruled from Jerusalem, but not from an easily recognizable throne or by a king who would be identified by the usual marks. The "times and seasons" are in God's control.

So they are told to wait. The very idea rubs us wrong. We are people of instant breakfast and get-up-and-go, get it done and come home to supper and that satisfied feeling of something *real* accomplished. But they are told to wait, even to "tarry" until they receive power. What all of this means, that they are to carry on his ministry as his witnesses, will become clear to them. Wait. As uncongenial as the idea may be to an activistic American, it is the only way to find out what we have and what we do not have.

Paul Tillich has said that "Waiting means not having and having at the same time."[1] Tillich launches into a kind of litany in which he urges us to be willing to wait with empty hands:

> I think of the theologian who does not wait for God, because he possesses Him, enclosed in a book. I think of the churchman who does not wait for God, because he possesses Him, enclosed in an institution. I think of the believer who does not wait for God, because he possesses Him, enclosed within his own experience.[2]

But the community which watches Jesus disappear out of their sight, waits. And in the waiting they discover what they do not have *and* what

1. Paul Tillich, *The Shaking of the Foundations* (New York: Charles Scribner's Sons, 1948), p. 149.
2. Ibid., p. 150.

they do have. Jesus is no longer present with them as he once was, but in his very absence they are brought together as people who rely on each other, and they are sent out as witnesses on a vast, new scale.

But we ought not to overlook the concreteness of this story. Even as we are being dazzled by the ascending Christ and commissioned to go to the ends of the earth, the writer maintains a dogged provincialism. These witnesses are to begin at Jerusalem. Wherever they go they will tell about the events that have occurred there. They are witnesses to Jesus who set his face to go to Jerusalem and was lifted up there to draw all persons to himself. Here is the particularity and the universality of the commission: Begin at Jerusalem and go as far as feet and beast and ship can take you. Even as Jesus leaves them, the place names which Luke records tie the church to this soil and to the deeds done here: Bethany, Jerusalem, Judea, Samaria, Olivet. As W. H. Auden has it:

> A poet's hope: to be,
> like some valley cheese,
> local, but prized elsewhere.[3]

". . . and in the act of blessing he parted from them." His going away is viewed here as part of the divine plan for the salvation of the world. Now the Spirit will come and they will understand more clearly what he meant and how they are to speak of him. The events of those last days in Jerusalem will become more and more meaningful as they experience together the reality of forgiveness and life together. So even as he leaves them, he blesses them. "And they returned to Jerusalem with great joy, and spent all their time in the temple praising God." There isn't anything about this that smacks of people standing on the platform or at the gate, to say nothing of the graveside, saying a last goodbye. His going away has made it possible for them to know just what they have, to bind them together, and to allow them no more leisure for gazing into heaven than reason for mourning his absence.

That painting, "Christ of St. John of the Cross," speaks of presence in absence. The cross is just suspended there, floating, and though Jesus is on it, there are no nails holding him there. We can see a long way and our view takes in sea and sky, sun, clouds and mountains, but everything we see is well within the view of the drooping—or is it soaring—figure on the cross. There is about even the black sky a peacefulness and the whole picture seems to hold together. Strange, though, how that can be: people working, a calm blue sea and azure sky, and the figure up there above it, not part of the scene below but not absent from it either. One thing is sure, looking at it we feel that we could easily, comfortably, cast the nets or set sail in the boat or walk along with the worker who lives under that ascending cross.

3. W. H. Auden, *Epistle to a Godson* (New York: Random House, 1969), p. 37.

The Seventh Sunday of Easter

Lutheran	*Roman Catholic*	*Episcopal*	*Pres./UCC/Chr.*	*Methodist/COCU*
Acts. 1:15-26	Acts.1:15-17, 20a, 20c-26	Acts 1:15-26	Acts 1:15-17, 21-26	Acts 1:15-26
1 John 4:13-21	1 John 4:11-16	1 John 5:9-15	1 John 4:11-16	1 John 4:11-16
John 17:11b-19	John 17:11b-19	John 17:11b-19	John 17:11-19	John 17:11-19

EXEGESIS

First Lesson: Acts 1:15-26. Several factors make clear that we have before us a speech composed by Luke, on the basis of earlier tradition to be sure, and quite appropriately placed in Peter's mouth: (1) v. 19: In the situation portrayed, Peter would scarcely need to inform the Jerusalem community of an event "known to all the inhabitants of Jerusalem," and he would certainly not interpret for such an audience an Aramaic expression, referring to Aramaic as "their language," that is to say, the language of Jerusalemites. It is Luke who, not having footnotes at his disposal, speaks to his Gentile readers, translating for them the Aramaic term. (2) v. 20: The interpretations of the Psalm texts (look them up!) presuppose the readings given in the Septuagint; they were made by persons in the Hellenistic church sometime prior to Luke's writing. Moreover, there were several traditions about Judas' death: note Matt. 27:3-10 (he hanged himself); Papias (he swelled to monstrous proportions). Luke has probably selected one from among those known to him. The statement of v. 17 is a piece of early Christian honesty and realism. There is no denying that Judas was one of the inner circle of the twelve.

This verse (17) is also one of the clues to Luke's interests and intentions. As we have seen repeatedly, Luke is keenly interested in the *linear continuity* of God's plan, as he causes it to be formed in the emergence of the great church. Hence, even a small share of "this ministry" cannot simply be dropped and forgotten. The church has a long way to go (1:18), and will need the full complement of its founding circle: Judas' place must be filled.

The requirements for the successor (vv. 21 f.) are the standards set in Acts for an apostle, and, again, these standards emphasize the need for continuity. This continuity is the product of God's acts, however, and is not the result of human "conservatism." That is made clear by the procedure followed to determine the successor's identity. There is no election, based on the principles of democracy ("the people rule"), which would have been, in fact, quite strange to the early church. God is the one who chooses, for the entire plan has been fixed by his authority (1:7). That this choice fell on a man named Matthias is known to Luke from tradition. The greatest weight falls on the continuity which links Jesus' life, Jesus' resurrection, and the "apostolic" ministry (witness) of the church (vv. 21-22). One may recall the three infinitives of Luke 24:46 f. The actions of God referred to in those infinitives, rather than any principle of organization, form the *fundamentum* of the emerging church.

Second Lesson: 1 John 4:13-21. Among the many motifs of this text, one of the most important is the statement about the mutually exclusive nature of Christian love and fear (4:18). The author lived in the Hellenistic age, one of the major marks of which was the widespread and dualistically oriented experience of anxiety. Indeed one might logically wonder whether a man who believes that "the spirit of deceit" is lurking about, seeking ways to lead folk astray into destruction (4:6), would not himself be subject to periods of fear. There is, in fact, every reason to believe that our author is personally acquainted with debilitating anxiety.

Yet he boldly affirms that love not only encompasses no fear, but also that love excludes fear from the field. How so? At least part of the answer lies in the link presupposed between fear (v. 18) and hatred (v. 20). Of whom might the author and his readers be afraid? In the first instance, perhaps, of the false teachers and of the spirit of deceit which animates the latter. But who are these teachers, precisely? They are the ones who say they love God, but hate their brothers. It seems that the author knows quite well that one hates because one is afraid. Hence the love which is perfected in the Christian fellowship is the antithesis of both hatred and fear.

Gospel: John 17:11b-19. This chapter presents the prayer of Jesus uttered virtually as though he were already in the process of ascending to the Father (vv. 11a, 12a, 13a). That will in itself remind us of the major *problem* to which the farewell discourses (chaps. 14-17) are addressed: Jesus Christ has come into the world which was created through him (1:3, 10); yet, paradoxically, the world does not, on the whole, welcome him (1:10; 12:37). To the world as such he is somehow The Stranger, and those who do believe in him become a community who are similarly strangers to the world (15:18 ff.; 17:14). Well and good, so long as he is with them. But now the time has come for the Stranger to return to the Father, and hence the problem: With his departure, his followers are left behind in foreign territory as orphans (14:18). This turn of events is bound to strike fear into their hearts (14:1).

All elements of the farewell discourses are formulated with this problem in mind. Not least 17:9-19, the sub-unit of chap. 17 of which our reading is a part. Note v. 11a: Jesus is no longer in the world, but the disciples remain in the world, and although he might consider asking the Father to remove also them out of the world (v. 15), he does not do so. What does he ask? While he was with them, he guarded them (v. 12); now he asks the Father to do that (v. 11a), and specifically to keep them from the evil one.

How is this request to be fulfilled? First, by the fact that Jesus has given to the disciples the Father's word (v. 14). The Father will now "consecrate" them in this word (v. 17), i.e., he will make them holy, as he is holy (v. 11) and will thus guard them. Second, by the paradoxical fact that the disciples are now sent into the world in a way quite analogous to the way the Father sent the Son into the world. We see here, once again, that the expression "world" is used to refer both to the largely hostile environment experienced by the Johannine community (e.g., 16:1 f.) and to the object of God's love and redemptive intentions. Note carefully 17:20 f. The Johannine community is not a collection of the last believers! There will certainly be others, and these others will believe because the apparent "orphans" are not left desolate, but are rather kept in God's word, and in fact are empowered by the coming of the Paraclete to utter that word to others.

HOMILETICAL INTERPRETATION

On this Sunday after the Ascension, close to Pentecost, we see the church in its germinal and seminal stages. What is private becomes provincial and then, in the confident power of the ascended Lord and the coming Spirit, becomes universal. In the Gospel for today, Jesus prays for his own little band. Luke tells of the community that has grown to the size of a modest parish church, and the Johannine epistle stakes out even larger territory. What has occurred in the environs of Jerusalem leaves the world different as these witnesses spread in all directions like ripples from one stone.

John 17:11b-19. Can we make too much of the power of a discrete human event? Is it true that what is most personal is most universal? We may be impressed by big scale and shiny ideology, but what is it that empowers these early Christians and keeps them going, uncowed by the power of Rome and the unbelieving hostility which they will face?

John shows us Jesus in retreat with the twelve, getting them ready to move out of the upstairs room and into the streets. He is washing their feet! It is a preparation for the sabbath. A group of friends are together for a meal of fellowship. At Jesus' hands the simple food and the washing become the sanctifying of a new sabbath, preparation for their role in God's new time which will be measured from the day of resurrection. As Jesus teaches his disciples, prays for them, and consecrates himself, he is equipping a cadre.

What great movement has not begun in privacy? And does not the church, into whatever streets it moves, find its origins and continuing identity by reference to the events of that room and immediately surrounding it? Behind the church at the barricades and rushing to the place where the action is, there is the church in retreat with the one who breaks bread and takes a towel. The Fourth Gospel gives ample room, indeed makes essential, what Marriane Moore calls "our particular possession, the sense of privacy." Elton Trueblood, too, calls the activist church, the public person, the leader, to the essential preparation of private experience. Jesus' last gift to those whom he will send into the world even as the Father has sent him, is to get them *away* from the world by a gift of intimacy.

What will, after all, hold them together? How is it possible that these men who have already shown themselves contentious, ambitious, and shallow could stay together, to say nothing of their carrying on Jesus' ministry? He prays for them: "Holy Father, keep them in thy name which thou hast given me, that they may be one, even as we are one." What we might expect here is a pep-talk or some good advice on sales technique or surefire evangelism. Instead, Jesus gives them gifts which they will not forget, the same gifts which they are to give. In the single act of washing their feet he both consecrates himself and sanctifies them. From such a seminal moment everything issues, and it is a moment which we easily recognize from our own experience. It didn't seem particularly important at the time, but it was that day when your mother came into your room for a talk, or your father kept a promise, or you received the letter. And the ripples are still going. And from time to time you remember that moment, and you place yourself by it as if it were one of those colored arrows on a map telling you "You are here."

What makes the church possible? What makes a family possible or, for that matter, enables one human life to hold together? What enables people to say "yes" to each other and to themselves and over the long haul to accept and affirm and stick with each other? The word "consecrate" is a sacrificial word. Jesus consecrates himself, gives himself up, and takes upon himself all that there is in human life which separates and says no and tears apart. And it is right there, in that washing of their feet. He consecrates himself, and the world is overcome, and the community of grace is born. As Jesus bends to them with the basin, there is a microcosm of all he meant and of all that his followers would become. Jesus' offering of himself becomes vine and door, true life and way. The friends who gather on that evening to sanctify the sabbath are themselves sanctified for the kingdom, sanctified not by virtue of their own perfectibility or competence but by the Lord whose self-sacrifice they know for themselves.

We can't make too much of the discrete event, of the particular story which we know, of what has happened to us. If we could ask any one of those men, later on, in who knows what circumstances: "Why do you speak as you do? How can you go on? Are you sure of what you are doing?", what would he say? Is Frederick Buechner right, that finally all of us have to push back our chairs and take off our spectacles and tell a story about something that happened to *us* once? Jesus has washed their feet and then sent them out without an extra pair of shoes to witness to the whole world. If we were to fish around for something like that experience today we would probably come up with a teacher or an artist "blowing our minds" and sending us out with only a pair of blue jeans and something to tell. Is that what it is like to overcome the world and to have his joy fulfilled in us?

Acts 1:15-26. Frost has it right, so far as Christianity is concerned. Swinging high on birches is fine, he says, within limits:

> May no fate willfully misunderstand me
> And half grant what I wish and snatch me away
> Not to return. Earth's the right place for love:
> I don't know where it's likely to go better.[1]

How many student ministers have lived, so to speak, way up in the birches on a seminary campus, only to find themselves on a weekend brought down to earth by people in a little country church with no indoor plumbing and a morning service that sometimes smelled more of people just in from doing the chores than of incense? Coming as we are now to the end of Eastertide, we are being brought down to earth. That is as it should be. The pattern in the NT is familiar: tarrying on the mountaintop is tolerated no more than gnostic tendencies to spiritualize the gospel.

From Olivet the disciples return to the room upstairs. The ascension of Jesus had been punctuated by an admonition: "Men of Galilee, why stand there looking up into the sky?" That we have seen God's glory shining forth in Jesus leads us down from the mountain and into the world of strategies. We remember the high moment, and we may even feel a pang when we take down the Christmas wreath in the middle of January, but finally we are brought back to our familiar places and mundane responsibilities. One of our best preachers, whose strength is his earthiness, says that we should always try to keep in mind that the church is just around the corner from St. John of the Gas Station. The room upstairs provides us a good symbol of both the mountain and the mundane. It is the place of the towel and the basin and dusty feet, of simple food and friends eating together. At the same time, it is much more, a transfiguration. But finally it is still bread and wine and human feet, common things which carry this meaning.

And so we see these early Christians, in the lees of the Ascension, turning to the election of a successor to Judas. There is about it something of the demeanor of the woman who goes to work the day after she wins the million dollar lottery or the man who cleans the gutters to celebrate a promotion. They name Matthias to succeed Judas, and we know that we have here to do with the *church*.

1 John 4:13-21. So here is the church which Jesus sanctified? Already they are fighting and threatened. The pastor is obviously appealing for community rather than contention, for the people to be together despite their differences and to live together in peace despite all that works against peace. Can it be? Can the lordship of the ascended Christ and the image of the footwasher bind these people? That is the only reassurance the writer offers: being together is a gift of God through Christ.

The images of family and home might work, as we try to get inside the

1. Robert Frost, "Birches," *Poems of Robert Frost* (New York: Modern Library, 1946), p. 128.

writer's understanding of Christian discipleship and community. Children growing up in a house learn quite early that the complex interconnections that make up "home" are held together by gifts. Oh, it's true that a house works better if everyone has duties and if certain limits are established. But finally "home" is unconditional free gift. This gift comes as many gifts, but the most significant are from the parents: the decision to have the child in the first place, the provision of food and toys and heat and light, and the tacit recognition by everyone in the house that these gifts may in fact be taken for granted. And that they are taken for granted is grounded in one fact, the love of human beings for each other. Home holds together in a house because people are *in* love. It is all the gift of love.

John paints such a picture of the Christian community. "God is love, and he who abides in love abides in God, and God abides in him." If we give the most universal interpretation to that verse, then we have reached the outermost boundary of the meaning of the ascension. John's intention is much more limited: the love we know, we know in Jesus Christ, and it is because of the love which we have seen in him that we are able to be together. John's pastoral advice could easily have for its text the story of Jesus washing his friends' feet, for the best gifts we have to give are those given to us.

My friend and I took a walk one spring morning, the kind of day when promises are easily made. He was feeling down, and the flowering magnolia tree we had left our chores to see must have been to him both joy and pain. "I will send you something," I said, as we walked back to our duties. "It is an essay by Oscar Wilde." "Fine," he said. He went home to Pennsylvania, time passed, and the promise and presence of mind and the book seemed never to get together, and there was that vague feeling of guilt not quite strong enough to move the laggard feet to the library. Then one day, I got down my friend's own book to prepare for class, and there it was as the book fell open, the very paragraph from Wilde's *De Profundis*. And I wrote to tell him: "My gift to you is your gift to me."

Set on the road, called to wash each other's feet, to forgive and bear with each other and be honest and stay at it, we have had our feet washed. And so we are able to love because he first loves us.